LEARNING TO LIVE AGAIN

A WIDOW'S JOURNEY TO JOY

LEARNING TO LIVE AGAIN

A WIDOW'S JOURNEY TO JOY

ROBBIE STEELE MARTIN

Copyright © 2023 by **ROBBIE STEELE MARTIN**

All rights reserved. No part of this book may be reproduced, distributed or transmitted in any form or by any means, without prior written permission of the copyright owner, except for the use of brief quotations in a book review.

To request permissions, contact the publisher at RobbieSteeleMartin@gmail.com.

Scriptures marked KJV are taken from the KING JAMES VERSION (KJV): KING JAMES VERSION, public domain.

Edited, Cover and Layout by Zelda Miles & byZeldaO, LLC
Cover and Author Photographs by Hollery Morris Photography

Learning to Live Again/ Robbie Steele Martin. -- 1st ed.
ISBN 979-8-89184-058-4 (paperback)

Published by Robbie Steele Martin

DEDICATION

This book is dedicated to My Dude, Rockets and Rock Star.

To My Dude, those two eyes that made my world better and filled my heart with love. Those two eyes that went to sleep before we were ready, prepared or willing to accept your absence from our presence. True love stories like ours never end.

To Rockets and Rock Star, the four eyes that look at me and I see love, grace, hope, adventure, and joy. Thank you for being you – for growing, evolving, learning, enjoying life and reminding me that joy is all around us. I marvel at your conscious choices to be better not bitter. I love you more than I can ever express, even when you call me Bruh and Linda!

Mine

I am my beloved and my beloved is mine

My lover,

My Dude,

My Boo & My Bae,

My friend, my confidante

My travel companion,

My personal tech support,

My football rival, my foot massager,

TEAM MARTIN

My shoe shopper, my huge shoulder to cry on

My protector, my provider, my life,

My world.

As each sun sets I will remember the many we watched together

And yet remains four beautiful eyes of reflection

In them I will see your compassion & your love

I am my beloved and my beloved is mine.

Eternally Yours in Victory,

Robbie

ACKNOWLEDGEMENTS

This book has been a journey of healing for me, but for those on the authorship journey with me, it has been a journey of faith, love (sometimes tough love), grace, being pushy, getting in my business, frustration, prayer, perspective and joy. For all who walked this journey with me, I thank God for you and I am appreciative. This is the Lord's doing and I marvel at it.

Mom and Dad – I wish you could see this. I have so many things I want to tell you. I think you always knew this was in me. Thank you for teaching me, not just with words but actions.

Verdel – My Dude, our love story will never end!

Jon and Kait – My kids, my constants, my reasons – my heartbeats. Thank you for listening, encouraging, being patient, being consistent, laughing, and celebrating. The pride and joy you displayed after seeing the book, made my heart swell. Knowing you are proud of me is priceless.

Grandma – My first insight to a widow, up close and personal. How you did what you did? Purchasing a home, maintaining you life, being and becoming. I thank God for your life everyday.

To my family – Thank you for your love and prayers. Life's journey has given us some easy roads and some mind-bogglingly, challenging roads. We all have our own way of navigating, learning, adjusting and just dealing. Grateful we have each other.

Bestie – You have a way of knowing when I need a shoulder to cry on, when I need coffee or ice cream and when I need the swift get-it-together kick. I guess that's what hearts knitted together do.
I love you.

The Ten – These ten figurative walked with me on the writing journey. God told me who to share my assignment with and I listened. Throughout this journey these ten prayed with me and for me. Checking on me and the book's progress. Asked me hard questions and reminded me of God's assignments to me when I got distracted or doubted, which was a real struggle. I am grateful for your strength, courage and wisdom. We did it y'all! God did it!

My godparents – Prayers, encouragement, laughter, grace, insight and the grounding statements "Let your heart lay down in Jesus," "God knows what lies ahead, and 'Hold it in the road." Thank you for loving me and mine.

My sister – Practical and protective, perspective shifting, loves hard and don't play the radio – I needed all of it. I thank you and salute you for being authentic.

Team Bivins –Team Bivins loves Team Martin. "We will get through this." The way you all have shown up in our lives is indescribable.

My godsisters – For never allowing me to drown in my sorrow and grief. Thank you for texts, jokes, lunches, dinners, getting me out of the house and out of my own way! I love y'all!

Bethesda Apostolic Worship Center – God is love. Love is kind. We are the Kind House. What's love got to do with this? Everything.

Carew Prayer Ministry – To know that I am prayed for daily and loved is an undeserved gift.

Stephanie – My sister from another mother. So much history. So many memories. So many "yes you cans." Thanks Suh!

Cher – You are not just my stylist, but my friend, supporting and praying for my every endeavor, speaking positively and declaring God's healing and blessing through this book. Thank you for creating the sisterhood of Cher's Angels. I love y'all and our walk for Christ.

The Late Bishop Heron Johnson — How I miss you! "Robbie, don't be ordinary, be extraordinary." Continuing to understand this assignment, and forever grateful for your love and wisdom.

Verdel's Forever First Lady Betty Bender — You loved unconditionally. You understood without questions through your bond with Verdel and us. You never allowed us to feel forgotten. We adore you.

Last, but not least, Zelda – the midwife of this book! The pushes, the pulls, the challenges, the grace, the guidance, the authenticity, the creativity, the prayers and the love. Thank you for editing this book and so much more. If they only knew how God did this!

Contents

Preface 2

Introduction 5

1 | Why Not Me? 9

2 | Full Circle 18

3 | True Love Stories Never End 24

4 | The Effect of Impact 35

5 | Mind Your Business, Please 46

6 | Grace to Grieve 58

7 | Triggers, Unwelcome Visitors 66

8 | Dancing in the Rain 72

9 | Glimmering, Glowing and Celebrating 78

10 | Are You Ready? 82

11 | Reset and Recovery 91

12 | The Dating Lane 99

Bonus | Thriving During Holidays and Special Occasions 109

STEELE MARTIN

Preface

I am a widow, but I am not waiting to live.

I am going to live while I wait.

I'm not sure if I am in waiting anyway.

It doesn't take a spouse to live. It takes a desire to live.

It doesn't take a date to live. It takes courage and strength to live.

It doesn't take an if and when to live. It takes a the when is now to live.

It takes you trusting God to heal your heart.

It takes grace and grit.

It takes memories and choices.

It takes you moving forward one day at a time to enjoy life and live again.

Yes loves, you are yet alive.

Choose to live. Choose joy.

— by *Robbie Steele Martin*

LEARNING TO LIVE AGAIN

A letter from your daughter's heart

Dear God,

As I looked at the cover of this book for the first time all I could do was weep. I am in absolute awe at how great you have been to me and my family. In miraculous fashion, with the love of the Father, you took an angry, brokenhearted widow, walked her through grief, anger, pain and fear; strengthened her faith, empowered her to do the work of recovery, and not only sustained, but moved her and her children forward to joy. Then you gave instructions to share her journey with others. That seems impossible. But I am that widow, so I know it's true.

Thank you for healing me. Thank you for healing us. Thank you for not leaving us. Thank you for walking on this journey with us. Yes, I am the same daughter that refused to talk to you after Verdel's death. Then anger, fear, anxiety, pain and grief seemed to be my portion. But God, you were there. You stayed when I pushed you away, you stayed when I yelled, you stayed when I pouted. You were strength like no other during the fiercest storm of my life. The very thing that I thought was going to take me out, you used to show your power, get the glory, and give us the victory.

I love that your love didn't leave us in despair. I love that you are greater than any grief. I love that the power of your word still consoles and heals. I love that I can still trust you with my heart. I love that you intentionally orchestrated encounters to show your unfailing love for us. I love that you are just there, even on days when we hurt and you give us strength to keep going.

I did not think that I would love you again God, but I do.

I do not know what lies ahead, but I know you have been so far beyond faithful that I trust you for our now and our next. I believe I understand why Jude penned chapter 1, verses 24 and 25 (KJV), "Now unto him that is able to keep you from falling, and to present you faultless before the presence of his glory with exceeding joy, To the only wise God our Saviour, be glory and majesty, dominion and power, both now and forever."

God, you are amazing!

Your joyful daughter,

Robbie

Introduction

Joy disrupts and interrupts grief. The power of joy can break the heaviness and strength of grief. The stinging pain of grief is soothed by joy. From grief, joy illuminates a path forward. It is joy that drives the will and desire to live again. I invite you to take a faith leap with me and journey from grief to joy. You may find that this journey is not pretty or neat, but if you take the leap, I believe you will find joy and live again.

Grief enters our lives without invitation, unwelcome. It arrives in moments of profound loss, when the world shatters into a thousand pieces. The heartbreaking and immediate absence, silent ache in the middle of the night, the empty chair at the table, and memories that once warmed our hearts suddenly birth anxiety, pain and tears.

Before I turned fifty, through death, I said goodbye to my parents, one of my dearest friends, and my beloved husband. It seemed the weight of all these losses was going to consume me. But I refused to let these losses and grief define and defeat me. I refused to be a casualty of grief. Rather, I went on a journey that led me through unfathomable grief, pain, processes, evaluations, rediscovery, and ultimately healing. I am grateful that this journey wasn't without moments of laughter and levity. While there were tears, there were also moments of pure hilarity like me trying to manually open the garage door during a power outage or navigating the weird world of dating.

My background is not in therapy or counseling. I, like many, found myself thrust into a world of grief that was bewildering. I searched for a map that wasn't there. While grieving for my husband, I scoured bookshelves and websites, looking for comfort, hope, and guidance. However, the resources I wanted were hard to come by. I wrote this book for people who wondered, like me, if they would ever return to a fulfilling life, to joy.

In the pages that follow, I invite you into my world—a world where grief isn't the end of the story, but rather a passage and bridge to the next chapter. It's a world where faith, love, resilience, hope, trust in God and family bonds become the pillars of the new landscape of life. Together, we'll explore the lessons I've learned along this challenging journey, lessons that have shaped me into the woman I am today.

Whether it's the loss of a loved one, the loss of marriage/relationship, the loss of direction, or the loss of self, this book is for you. It's for those who need a guide through the labyrinth of grief. You're the one who has stared into the abyss of pain and wondered if you'd ever get out. I have good news: you will.

As I share my stories, reflections, and insights, I hope you'll find strength, hope, a renewed sense of purpose, and even a good laugh. My story isn't just about me; it's about how God helps us to endure, heal, thrive, and even find humor in the darkest moments.

Together, let's navigate grief's unpredictable journey. Though we may not have chosen this path, we can choose how we walk it. And through that choice, we discover hope, strength, beauty, and joy. Welcome to a journey from grief to joy, exploring faith, purpose, unexpected laughter, and moments that help light the way. Welcome to a world where joy transcends the darkest of days. Welcome to living again.

> *"Trust in the Lord with all thine heart; and lean not unto thine own understanding. In all thy ways acknowledge him, and he shall direct thy paths." Proverbs 3:5-6 (KJV)*

> *"Happy is the man that findeth wisdom, and the man that getteth understanding." Proverbs 3:13 (KJV)*

I want to share with you the worship that kept my heart and mind as I wrote this book:

>What heights of love
>What depths of peace
>Where fear are stilled
>Where striving cease
>My Comforter
>My All In All
>Here in the love of Christ I stand
>In Christ the Lord my hope is found
>He is my light, my strength, my song
>This cornerstone, this solid ground
>Firm through the fiercest drought and storm
>What heights of love
>What depths of peace
>When fears are stilled
>Where striving cease
>My Comforter
>My All In All
>Here in the love of Christ I stand
>No power of hell
>No scheme of man
>Can ever pluck me from His hands
>'Til He returns or calls me home
>Here in the power of Christ I stand
>No guilt in life
>No fear in death
>For this is the power of Christ in me
>From life's first cry
>'Til final breath
>Jesus commands my destiny
>
>Victor Thompson Music, No Power of Hell
>(YouTube July 17, 2022)

1 | Why Not Me?

10.10.2016 — the day my life and my family landscape changed forever. The day my husband, my beloved, my Dude, my Verdel died.

In the days following my husband's death, grief and life blurred together. Family and friends rallied around us, providing comfort, condolences, and casseroles. It was overwhelming to get so many messages of love, and for those moments, it reminded me I wasn't alone. People's kindness defied boundaries. Everything from food to flowers, gift cards to gift trips, donated work vacation days to a bank account set up for the kids was given to us.

It was a challenge explaining Verdel's passing to our kids, who at the time were twelve and fourteen. I was grateful they had visited their father the previous day and were able to talk, laugh, and enjoy each other as only the three of them could, making so much noise and racket. I feared we would be asked to leave, but God knew what was ahead. As I talked to them about God's will and sovereignty, explaining to them that we were having a lesson in quality over quantity. Even though their time with their father had been cut short, in our eyes, they had experienced fullness, profound moments of love and teaching, and memories for a lifetime. They already knew their father was an amazing man, however, now every word and memory of their father was a priceless treasure.

Jon and Kait were devastated by the news of their father's passing, but their responses reminded me that Verdel had planted in good ground. "Mom, he's not here physically, but he will always be in our hearts. He lives there now," Jon said.

Funeral arrangements, legal matters, and notifying friends and family kept me occupied days after Verdel passed. While I was busy, grief constantly washed over me, leaving me breathless and drowning in sadness. At night, the stillness of the house and the empty space at the table, and my solo trips to bed were constant reminders of Verdel's absence. But I held on to my faith in mourning. My faith was my lifeline. There were countless times Verdel and I prayed together, seeking guidance and strength. Our faith was central to our relationship, and now was my solace.

God is so intentional. During the days, weeks and early months after Verdel's death, I was surrounded by family, inner circle friends, neighbors and co-workers. My sister was my constant companion. I remember one of my friends from Jamaica flew to Alabama after learning of Verdel's death. Toya stayed at my home for more than a week. She is a true woman of prayer, an intercessor. Every time I saw her, she was praying –

in the kitchen, the family room, the kids' rooms. She prayed in every room in our home. I am forever grateful!

Our dear friend and now pastor came to our home the day after Verdel died. I knew he was at the house, but I couldn't find him there were so many people there. When I did find him, he was walking the perimeter of our home, praying. After walking, he stood by the light in the backyard and prayed some more. It's been over seven years and that light has not gone out. God intentionally sent who we needed.

I remember one afternoon after the children had returned to school and my companions had returned to their lives, I lay on my living room floor, kicking, screaming, weeping in agony, tears, and grief. I screamed at God, "WHY ME? WHY DIDN'T YOU TAKE SOMEBODY ELSE'S HUSBAND. SOMEBODY WHO DOESN'T LOVE THEIR HUSBAND. SOMEBODY WHO DOESN'T WANT TO BE MARRIED AND DOESN'T CARE! WE LOVED VERDEL AND HE LOVED US.

God kindly said, "Why not you Robbie?"

"I can't do this," I said.

"So, are you saying I can't keep you and bring you through this?" God lovingly asked me.

"No, I just don't want to. I don't know how. God, I feel like you ripped out my heart and told me to go on," I said in tears.

"I told you to trust me. If you trust me, I will keep you. I will never leave you. I am going to get the glory out of this because you loved each other and you love me," God said to me.

Sobbing, I said, "This is really real. My husband is gone."

God was telling me to trust Him. How was I supposed to trust God when I didn't like Him? I was angry because I had begged, pleaded, cried, bargained with God and He still chose to take my husband and my children's father.

God took what was His. Yes, Verdel was mine in the earth, but Verdel belonged to God in earth, in heaven, and in eternity. Verdel belonged to God first and last. God was absolutely within His sovereignty to end Verdel's life when and how He chose to. I was angry because I didn't get my way. I knew God was sovereign and that He could have, but He choose not too. That hurt so much. Then on top of hurting me and those I love the most, God had the audacity to tell me to trust Him. You've got to be kidding me. You already broke my heart after I trusted you with it in marrying Verdel. "God," I cried, "if you were going to do this, you could have left me single. Why would you do this to Jon and Kait?" I felt I had every right to be angry, God had already taken my mother and my father, both of my parents were only children — so no Aunts or Uncles for me. God you have taken everyone that I depend on and lean on. As angry as I was, God still said "trust me, depend on me, lean on me." It was like God said, "I got y'all, just keep going."

Finality. God said again, "trust me, I am with you." At some point, I got off the floor, dried my eyes and said, "okay God, I guess we are really doing this. I don't have much to say to you. I'm so angry at you, but you are the only one who can help me."

I didn't want to talk to God, but I knew I needed to talk to Him because this was too much for me. Some days I talked to God, some days I only wept to Him. Some days I intentionally said nothing to God.

I realized, in spite of my pouting and my refusing to talk to God, that God was being faithful to the word He spoke to me. God was with us. God was helping us. God changed the landscape of my life and had given me assurance. He was actively and daily helping us while we grieved. It was up to me to trust Him. I felt like I was drowning and that my world had completely stopped. I realized that no matter how much I cried or how much I didn't speak to Him, Verdel wasn't coming back. God had decided this is how it's going to be.

Somewhere in my tears a stirring of gratefulness was birthed. Gratefulness for God's grace during my pain, anger, and selfishness. I began to meditation on Psalms 147:3 (KJV), *"He healeth the broken in heart, and bindeth up their wounds."* I had no idea about the journey ahead, but I knew God said that He would be with us. Joshua 1:9 (KJV), is now one of my favorite scriptures: *"Have not I commanded thee? Be strong and of a good courage; be not afraid, neither be though dismayed for the Lord thy God is with thee whithersoever thou goest."*

Because God said He would be with us, I knew we did not have to be a casualty of grief. I was going to operate in His power and strength and not my own. This realization did not happen overnight, it was and has been a process. Along the way there were days that looked like total defeat, but God always came through for us. I believe we became totally dependent on Him for our help and our hope because we wanted to have joy again.

Sometime later, I was reminded of something Verdel said while he was in the hospital. He told me hadn't just married me because I was beautiful, but because I was a strong, independent, smart, resourceful woman, who sometimes needed a step stool. (The man always had jokes about my height.) I realized that my life journey wasn't over. The tears came again. Verdel had plotted the course on the map and led the way, but it was my job to carry on TeamMartin's legacy of love, faith, and resilience. As Verdel wanted and as I realized, I had to be truthful, faithful, and mindful of the children.

Now with a newfound purpose, I set out on the healing journey. I faithfully attended my counseling sessions, which sometimes included a grief support group with the opportunity to share my pain and progress with others. I also started writing in my journal, pouring out my feelings and thoughts. I found it to be a cathartic process. I saw glimpses of God's plan as time passed. I often took to social media to share my thoughts about grief and hope. This became my platform to share my grief, faith, and healing journey. Two months after Verdel's death, I recall sharing the following experience on social media:

Verdel and I made a game of hiding each other's gifts in plain sight, like the closets, garage, and the pantry.

Apparently, I have been walking by these goodies for months. I discovered two Christmas wrapped gift boxes while cleaning up. I didn't know what or whose they were until I read the card: Merry Christmas, I love you forever, Verdel. This moment completely took my breath away. I can't fully explain how I feel. Overwhelmed with love and grateful to God are the best I can give right now. Definitely another sit down moment. Well, I closed the box without peeking, and put these babies right under the tree. My Dude thought of everything. Thank you Lord. God always knows and Verdel got me again.

Later, I shared this:

I have thought about the present finding moment so many times. Sometimes with a smile, sometimes with tears. Today, God let me see this in a new light. God is so kind to us. God deals with us gently and lovingly, even in times when our world is upside down. God is patient, God reminds, reveals, helps, God is there. God didn't have to allow me to find these gifts when I did. God didn't have to allow Verdel to purchase them, but God knew what was ahead. When I initially found the gifts, I thought wow Verdel truly loved me until death. Now my thought is that God loves me enough to show me that He was carrying me, even in Verdel's death. God is a present help. God reminds us of His sovereignty. He cares about our pain, our sorrows, and our grief. God reminds us that He is with us, carrying us until we can stand and go forward on our own. God is there. Look for Him, sometimes it's the song in your mind, sometimes it's the word of a stranger, and sometimes it's that thing that happened to you that you can't explain other than to say it was God. Even in our pain, God is with us.

There was an overwhelming response to the posts from readers. People from all walks of life reached out, shared their stories, and asked for my advice. This experience was shared by so many and touched so many. That's when I realized the power of transparency and vulnerability. People looking for help and hope were asking me for advice and how to move forward. This pushed me out of my comfort zone. I began to share my private journey of grief. I had not found joy, but I knew if I kept going, I would find joy again. And I wanted to help anyone I could.

Somewhere along the way, I got involved in my church's bereavement ministry, where I was able to comfort and support people. My sense of purpose came from serving others. No longer was I just a mourner; I was a beacon of hope.

Through the years, I've continued to write, share my story, and support others through their grief. I found my purpose — to be a light for those in grief, a source of hope for those who are lost, and a testament to the strength of faith and love. I constantly found myself in situations orchestrated by God to share with others about my grief and loss. God, why me? Became Robbie, why not you?

And so, my journey continued, one step at a time, one day at a time, and one pair of shoes at a time. I knew God had a plan for me. It was my goal to walk out that purpose, just as Verdel had encouraged me and countless others during his illness.

As I write these words, I am reminded of my journey to joy. It is a journey of healing, of learning to navigate a world without the physical presence of the man I loved. But, it is also a journey of discovery, of uncovering the enduring power of love and the resilient power of hope. This is just a reminder that even in our darkest moments, there is a glimmer of light waiting to guide us to joy.

> *"Hast thou not known? Hast thou not heard, that the everlasting God, the LORD, the Creator of the ends of the earth, fainter not, neither is weary? There is no searching of his understanding. He giveth power to the faint; and to them that have not might he increaseth strength. Even the youths shall faint and be weary, and the young men shall utterly fall: but they that wait upon the LORD shall renew their strength; they shall mount up with wings as eagles; they shall run, and not be weary; and they shall walk, and not faint." Isaiah 40:28-31* (KJV).

2| Full Circle

In April 1998, I witnessed a display of strength that defied the human condition. My mother, a woman I had always known to be strong, powered by a godly, supernatural force, became the example of support during sorrow.

She and breast cancer were battling it out for the second time. Chemotherapy had taken her thick black hair and replaced it with gray curls. We thought chemo had taken her strength too. For an entire week, she lay in bed drained of appetite, energy, mobility, and vigor. It was a Friday night, and I got home late from work, preoccupied with trial preparation. I did not check my messages or caller ID when I arrived home. (This was before everyone had cell phones and text messaging.) One of the most devastating messages our family would ever receive sat in my inbox.

The message was from one of my best friends. Her message said that her father had collapsed at home, and they were at the hospital. It was extremely serious. The next morning when I listened to the message and called my dear friend, her father had passed away. The grief was twofold: my friend lost her father, but my mother's dear friend lost her husband.

Our connection was the church we attended, but love for each other's family bonded us during our work together. My friend and I worked with the young people and our mothers worked with the children. In addition to being a Sunday School teacher and Children's Church director, my mother was the director of Vacation Bible School at church. She was everybody's Momma. We were devastated, hysterical, and heartbroken over the news this death. I remember crying for a long time. I was still crying when my Momma said, "Robbie take me over there." I said, "Yes, ma'am we will definitely go over later in the week." She said, "No dear today." I said, "Momma, you've been in bed all week," to which she replied, "I've got to go today." She gave me "the Gwen Steele look." That's what I called the look she'd often give me; the look we now refer to as "side-eye."

"Yes, ma'am," I said and assisted her in getting dressed. Silence filled the almost thirty minute drive. At least I was silent. When I reflect back on this profound moment in her life, she was praying, interceding, talking to God and getting instructions from Him. I had no idea what I was about to witness, or the profound blessings I would receive eighteen years later.

There were two entrances to my friend's family home, either steps or a hill. Momma been in bed all week without eating and her legs were weak. Yet, she selected the stairs because the rails would offer support. I was anxious, fearing she would fall. As she cleared the first set of steps with my assistance, she rested on the landing before tackling the second set of steps.

Somewhere between that landing and the parlor entrance, God performed a miracle.

My Momma went from hunched over, breathless and dragging her feet to walking upright and breathing normally. I watched in awe as she moved unaided to her dear friend. I saw the moment their eyes and hearts connected, when my Momma's friend rose from her seat to meet my beloved Momma, who embraced her. She collapsed into my Momma's arms in grief, and she who barely was able to walk less than five minutes ago stood there, bearing both their physical weights, absorbing the emotional weight of her dear friend's grief, panic, and sorrow as she cried and releasing all the spiritual strength she had prayed for. Everyone knew my Momma was ill, but she stood there as God's vessel bearing, releasing, and interceding. I will never forget that moment.

On November 23, 1998, we bowed to God's will as my beloved mother passed away. The following year, in 1999, I married Verdel Martin. My mother's friend was an integral part of our wedding, present for the birth of our first child in 2002 and our second child in 2004.

Eighteen years later, in October of 2016, after my beloved husband's sudden death, my Momma's friend she walked into my house just as my Momma had walked into hers. She met me in the living room, embraced me tightly, and I crumbled and wept under the weight of my grief, pain, sorrow, disbelief, confusion, and panic. Just as my Momma had done for her, she bore our physical weight, taking on my emotional burdens and replacing them with God's peace and calm. We stood there for what seemed like hours. It was at that moment that I knew God was in my living room orchestrating a spiritual exchange, just as

He had been in her living room eighteen years ago bringing about divine transformation.

God's promises are unwavering, and I am so grateful He walks with us on this unpredictable life journey. Grief is a part of life. It has its own process, not entry, linger and depart. It's impossible to simply arrive at grief, spend a few moments there, and then leave. There are some losses that forever change the landscape of our lives. Processing these changes, accepting the new reality, learning to live again, and eventually experiencing joy takes time and trust. It's said grief proceeds in five stages, but every loss is different so there is no one-size-fits-all grieving process. We all experience loss differently. Each person is different, and each loss is different as well. It is important to remember that God is sovereign and walks with us on this journey.

There is only one constant in the midst of grief: God is present. In spite of the loss, process, and journey being different, God's word promises that He is present at all times. Here are some of God's promises that helped through my grief and loss. God promises that:

1. Psalms 34:18 (KJV) — God knows about your broken heart and is right there with you no matter what you feel — brokenness, despair, pain, or anger.
2. Hebrews 13:5 (KJV) — God said, He will never leave you or forsake you (especially in times of grief and sorrow). Grief can be so intense and gripping that the enemy would have us believe that God

cannot be with us in such a time of deep sorrow. But the enemy is a liar. God is faithful and His word is true.

3. Psalms 46:1-11(KJV) — In times of trouble, God is our refuge and strength, a very present help. The Psalmist declares that God is our safe place, our source, and always ready to help us. The Psalmist describes "times of trouble" as a time of destruction, changing landscapes and life-altering events. These events also describe the impact of a loved one's death on our lives and our emotional landscape. The Word of God declares, I am with you always — early, late, day, night, every moment, every hour, every day. Constant means continuously and always. God is present in every moment of your grief. *God says I met your grief and I'm greater than it. I was present before your grief arrived, God said. I was present when your grief arrived, and I will be present when it is defeated. I am your strength. I am your help, to bring you through grief to joy.*

God knew the grief was coming. Please know and remember that our grief is no match for our Savior.

Another full circle moment: Verdel moved to Alabama in April 1998 and was searching for a church he had seen on television. Unaware that the neighborhood the church was located in had two streets with the same name, he hadn't been able to locate the church. One Saturday, determined to find this church, Verdel began driving through the neighborhood and happened upon a long line of cars, a funeral procession. As he followed them, he found the church. Our church. The funeral procession was that of my friend's father. God's ways and promises are so amazing.

3 | True Love Stories Never End

One of the most exciting days of my life occurred on June 5, 1999. This day I married Verdel. He was the man I had prayed for, dreamt about, and waited for my entire life. Verdel was a tall, dark, and handsome gentleman.

As my bridesmaids and I were getting ready, the wedding coordinator's assistant walked into my dressing room in a panic. She informed me that there was a problem with the floral arrangements. My flowers were supposed to be lavender and my bridesmaids' flower were supposed to be white.

I recall smiling at her and asking, "Is Verdel here?" She said, "Of course." Then I asked, "Is Bishop here?" She said yes. I nodded and said, "I don't care who's not here. At four o'clock, open those doors so I can walk down that aisle." And just like that the man I had come to love, married Robbie, a spirited, shoe-loving lady from Alabama. What a pair we made!

Our love grew stronger over our seventeen years of marriage. We learned to love every facet of each other's personalities, no matter how challenging it was. We worked together, grew as individuals, humbles ourselves, learned to forgive, and understood the importance of apologizing. We weren't just willing; we actively engaged in the hard work of our marriage. Together, we became one.

When Verdel stepped into my life, I was in one of the most uncomfortable, confused, and warring states of my life. He'd become a member of my church, Faith Apostolic Church, but we hadn't met. Despite hearing the buzz, I had no idea who the young, single man was all the young women were talking about. At the time, I was focused on my mother, who was battling breast cancer for the second time, and my legal career, which had hit a pothole and appeared to be stalling or worse, derailing completely.

I had been hired by a good law firm, but assigned to a partner who refused to tell the truth. He lied so much that it was almost impossible to determine what was true or not. He had no regard for ethical standards or legal integrity. In my opinion, he was the worst boss ever. "Teflon man" is what my father called him because nothing stuck to him, his lies seemed to always work out in his favor. He made my life a living nightmare while I learned a lot on my own like how not to treat people and how not to behave. That story doesn't need to be told here, just know, my God did not allow my boss's lies and reputation to mar mine.

Every day was a struggle for me. I felt like I was drowning at home and at work. I remember my godmother saying to me, "Robbie, you don't smile anymore. You always look sad." I kind of was. I did find great joy in seeing my baby nephew and niece.

As I stated earlier, my mother was battling breast cancer. She'd been diagnosed when I was in high school and had mastectomy. She was that told because her lymph nodes were clear and the cancer had been successfully removed, she didn't need radiation or chemotherapy. That was in 1986. If I knew then what I know now looking back, I would have insisted on at least some radiation, but we didn't know we could have requested preventative radiation, or chemotherapy. Her adult-onset asthma was one of the factors we considered, and we were grateful that the surgery was all this cancer required.

In 1995, however, the cancer returned to my mother's body, initially seemingly isolated, and then spreading. By 1998, when I met Verdel, my mother was in a full-blown fight for her life, and you can be sure I was doing everything I could to help her fight. I was praying, believing, and trusting God as we confronted this formidable foe. Meanwhile, my legal career crumbled under my unscrupulous boss' lies.

The kick-off to my and Verdel's love story began when my godsister orchestrated a meeting between the two of us. They believed we were a perfect match. Despite my initial skepticism, our paths crossed and the rest became our never-ending love story.

Fourteen months later, seven months after my mother's passing, we became Mr. and Mrs. Verdel Martin. Verdel often likened us to a kite — the kite and its string — flying high together. He was "My Dude" and I was "His Girl." God blessed us with two wonderful children. Everything seemed better with Verdel. My career was flourishing, and even when a problematic leader and colleague made advances toward Verdel, leading to my job loss we relied on our faith in God.

I consider myself a peaceful woman, but that day in the office, I was ready to fight ten rounds with that audacious colleague. She had the nerve to ask if my husband could take her to the airport. Such blatant disrespect triggered a fire within me. Though I was not one to engage in fights, I was prepared to make an exception. To my relief, later she ultimately paid the price for her behavior.

I firmly believe that I became a better person through our marriage. This is not simply because I was a wife, but because I was Verdel's wife. One of the most profound moments of our marriage occurred during one of our "lively discussions." Verdel noticed I was not listening, but formulating my response. He told me, "Rob, we're on the same team. Don't listen to respond. Listen to understand." Those words fundamentally changed how I engaged with people and influenced the creation of our family mantra, "TeamMartin."

We faced numerous challenges, celebrated successes, and navigated life together. We braved racial tensions in our workplaces and children's schools. We endured heartbreak, heartache, and unexpected circumstances. When faced with unemployment and Verdel's cancer diagnosis, we stood united.

Then suddenly, while we were doing life, Verdel got seriously ill. Two weeks later, I found myself standing in a hospital's intensive care unit trying to comprehend that my beloved husband had peacefully passed away. In my anguish, I cried out to God, asking about our children, his family, friends, and myself. I thought God had chosen me to be Verdel's wife, and I was devoted to that calling. I served God with all my heart, mentored young people and women's groups, and started a blog, as He instructed. Although I hadn't finished my book, I had taken the firs steps. I thought I understood my purpose, but at that moment, I questioned it all.

Returning home after Verdel's passing, three precious young women helped me get into bed. I remember closing my eyes hoping to sleep, but feeling as if life was leaving my body. One of the most painful, selfish, authentic, raw moments of my life was awakening the next morning to realize the world had not stopped, that the sun was up, and that people were carrying on with their lives. How in the world had everything in the world not come to complete stop? My husband, my love, my babies' daddy, my dude had passed away. How was the world going on like nothing had happened? I could feel rage, but I also heard an annoying sound.

The sound was someone ringing my doorbell at seven o'clock in the morning. As I stumbled through my house, I tripped over people asleep on the floor, chairs, and couches. Nevertheless, I opened the door and my neighbor from around the corner, who was also my children's assistant principal was standing there. Her husband had passed away a few years earlier. She grabbed me and hugged me with tears falling from her eyes, she said something and left. Later, she told me it was all she knew to do, and she had come over as soon as she found out about Verdel's passing. I don't know how she knew, maybe school media, because we hadn't contacted the school. Regardless, God knew what I needed because I had told myself I wasn't getting up ever again.

As you can imagine, I was weary with grief and deep in sorrow. My world had crashed and I would never be able to put it back together the way it had been. Weariness transitioned into exhaustion because I had to work hard to keep things as normal as possible for my children so they didn't spiral into depression. On some evenings, I would come home, sit on the bed to take off my shoes and fall asleep for hours, but I was grateful for the sleep.

It was shortly after I went to get my annual women's checkup that a turning point occurred for me. My doctor's office was located in the same hospital where my husband passed. I had intentionally avoided driving near that area because I couldn't bear to be near the hospital. As you can imagine, I had rescheduled this appointment until my doctor called and said, "Robbie, keep this appointment. I need to see you."

On this particular morning, I talked to myself, prayed, sang, and worshipped God. I got dressed and headed to the doctor's office. I made it to the hospital without falling apart. But, I forgot I had to park in the same parking deck and walk across the same crosswalk that months before I had sprinted across to get to my husband the day he died. As I walked across that crosswalk, tears streamed down my face. By the time I got to the elevators, I was bawling. When I reached my doctor's office, I was on the verge of hyperventilating. The nurses rushed me to the back, gave me some water, and let me lay down until the doctor was ready to see me.

When my doctor comes in, I was a complete wreck. An utter mess, shallow breathing, stomach cramps, disheveled and makeup running everywhere. She says to me, "Robbie, I thought you were doing better. We are going to have to give you something because you can't continue like this. You can't function like this." She wrote me prescriptions for anxiety and depression and made me promise I would get them filled. And, I did. I remember looking at the medicine bottles and thinking "how did I get here?"

A couple of days later, I had another episode, this time I was crying but there were no tears or sound. I decided to take one of the pills. It knocked me out for hours. When I woke up even more anxious, disoriented and unsteady, I realized had hit the bottom. Grief had taken over my life. I was feeling lost, lonely, overwhelmed, and weary. In that moment, I clearly remember saying to God, "I have told so many people that you are a keeper, a comforter, and a deliverer. I know you to be those things. God, I need you to heal me and help me to make it, not on these medicines, but by faith in you." Literally, I cried out to God with everything in me and said, "God I don't know how to go on."

(Disclaimer: I am not against medication. Grief, I've come to understand, can disrupt one's hormones and chemical balance. They just didn't work for Robbie. I knew my healing had to come through a different process.)

Now, I was also struggling with my own guilt, thoughts, and opinions as well as those of others. I thought God "short-changed" my children. I felt guilty about being alive. I felt

Verdel was the better person and parent, so how was it that I was the one remaining? Verdel was the leader of our family, and I was honored to follow him, so how was I the one remaining. In addition to my own thoughts and guilt, I had been asked "what I had done to Verdel?" prior to his death. This question sparked all types of emotions from rage to assault. But, I had to stop inflicting emotional self-pain. My self-pain added fuel to my already overwhelming grief.

    God said to me, "I didn't tell you that you would know how, I told you to trust me. Your purpose now is to let people see that I can keep you despite the pain from the death of your beloved husband. I am your keeper, I am with you. I have got you and I have got your kids, and I'm going to get the glory."

    Those words from God were the directional strength I needed to move forward on my journey without Verdel. I consistently continued counseling. I exercised. I learned. I listened. I shared. I was intentional. I cried. I was angry. I rested. I was honest with myself. I released the guilt of being alive. I quit quitting on God. I worked on becoming stronger than my grief. I took vitamins. I changed my diet. I pursued life and joy. Did I get it right every day? No. It's a journey, a process. Did I still have tears. Yes. The pain was still there, but I was trusting God past the pain. I began to understand a revelation Verdel shared with me while receiving cancer treatments. He said, "Robbie, you are looking at it the wrong way. It's an honor to be chosen by God as a vessel for Him to use for his glory, so I accept God's plan regardless."

As God said, my life and the lives of my children have brought Him glory. In spite of my loss, God gives me strength to write and speak about His awesome keeping power and love for me. Jon and Kait are both in college now. In the year their father passed, our amazing Kait, then in seventh-grade, made all A's and one B and was inducted into the Junior National Honor Society. In the same year, Jon, a ninth-grader and track athlete, broke several freshman records, and was a part of one of the top high school relay teams in the nation. Were are their days wonderful? No. They had some painful, sorrowful, ugly days. But they decided they would keep going. They lived, they grew, and they adjusted. I am thankful for their amazing village. I am thankful that they chose to be better not bitter.

In the midst of my grief and the chaos that had engulfed my life, God revealed that my purpose was to show others that He could sustain me, even after losing my beloved husband. I had to trust God beyond my pain, and I understood that my purpose wasn't solely about me; it was about bringing glory to God. Pain and purpose ain't always about us.

> *"And he said unto me, My grace is sufficient for thee: for my strength is made perfect in weakness. Most gladly therefore will I rather glory in my infirmities, that the power of Christ may rest upon me."* 2 Corinthians 12:9 (KJV)

> *"Nay, in all these things we are more than conquerors through him that loved us. For I am persuaded, that neither death, nor life, nor angels, nor principalities, nor powers, nor things present, nor things to come, Nor height, nor depth, nor any other creature, shall be able to separate us*

from the love of God, which is in Christ Jesus our Lord." Romans 8:37-39 (KJV)

"Having predestinated us unto the adoption of children by Jesus Christ to himself, according to the good pleasure of his will, To the praise of the glory of his grace, wherein he hath made us accepted in the beloved." Ephesians 1:5-6 (KJV)

The way Verdel lived taught me that being chosen by God to be a vessel through which He could receive glory was an honor. This means more than just praising God with our lips, but our behavior, our choices, and our everyday life was a source of praise to God. Despite my pain, I embraced that truth. God had plans to use me and my family to demonstrate His faithfulness and love to others.

What does our behavior communicate to God when we intentionally mope, pout, and refuse to move forward with our lives after someone dies? Do we remain ungrateful that He continues to bless us with life, goodness, and mercy every day? Have we resigned ourselves to the fact that life, joy, family, future and purpose have ended because of our loved one's death? Are we refusing to live out our purpose because we disagree with the sovereign God's decision? Are we suggesting that God cannot sustain us? Are we quitting on God, life, joy, the future, family, and purpose? What are you doing?

Walking with purpose means becoming more than a thermometer that gauges room temperature. It means becoming a thermostat, capable of measuring the atmosphere, influencing it, and changing the temperature. When we walk in purpose, we impact the world around us for the better just as God intended. How are you walking?

4|The Effect of Impact

Bishop Rick August of Biloxi, Mississippi, is one of my favorite people in the world. The warmth in his eyes and the compassion in his voice left a lasting impact on me when he said, "It's about impact. The impact of Verdel's life versus the impact of his death."

To us, he is more than a friend. Our children affectionately call him Uncle Ricky. Even with his wife in the hospital at the time of Verdel's passing, but with her love and blessing he came to Birmingham to see about us and stand by our side. He served as master of ceremony at Verdel's victory/homegoing celebration, which was nothing short of extraordinary. For those who may be wondering, in the Pentecostal community we refer to the funeral service as a "victory celebration" because through Jesus Christ's death, burial, and resurrection, we who have already experienced spiritual rebirth know that death has been conquered and we will live again.

> *"Now when they heard this, they were pricked in their heart, and said unto Peter and to the rest of the apostles, Men and brethren, what shall we do? Then Peter said unto them, Repent, and be baptized every one of you in the name of Jesus Christ for the remission of sins, and ye shall receive the gift of the Holy Ghost.*

> *39 For the promise is unto you, and to your children, and to all that are afar off, even as many as the Lord our God shall call." Acts 2:37-39 (KJV)*
>
> *"But I would not have you to be ignorant, brethren, concerning them which are asleep, that ye sorrow not, even as others which have no hope. For if we believe that Jesus died and rose again, even so them also which sleep in Jesus will God bring with him. For this we say unto you by the word of the Lord, that we which are alive and remain unto the coming of the Lord shall not prevent them which are asleep. For the Lord himself shall descend from heaven with a shout, with the voice of the archangel, and with the trump of God: and the dead in Christ shall rise first: Then we which are alive and remain shall be caught up together with them in the clouds, to meet the Lord in the air: and so shall we ever be with the Lord. Wherefore comfort one another with these words." 1 Thessalonians 4:13-18 (KJV)*

It seemed that impact was the word to describe this new season of my life. Many people, including strangers and co-workers, shared stories about the profound impact Verdel had on their lives. I knew my husband was special, but the encounters people described confirmed that God had been at work in his life. Verdel was undoubtedly a vessel of God.

One of Verdel's colleagues, Steve Johnson, shared a touching experience during the victory service. It is a story worth preserving. I'd like to share it with you:

Verdel was a great man and I feel so privileged to have been his friend. Verdel Martin became what I consider my best friend at Southern Company in Birmingham, AL. When Verdel was transferred into our IT group, we had adjoining cubicles. As we got to know each other better we became good friends. My wife, Jill, and I would often have lunch with Robbie and Verdel. We both had kids (although our kids were older, already young adults) and would share our stories and concerns. We supported Jon and Kait at their sports events and enjoyed watching them grow up.

As our Team Leader, Verdel would not talk about his illness much, it was very personal and private to him. The more we became friends, the more he would open up and share what was going on. I would at times call our work group together. We were all Christians and we would have prayer for Verdel. Verdel and I were always playing jokes on Robbie or telling jokes to Robbie, because we all worked for the same company, but different departments. Usually the joke was from something funny happening to me or Verdel or Verdel and I were pulling a prank on Robbie. We would call Robbie up on the speaker phone and tell her about it. We would have a good laugh between the three of us.

I remember one day I came to work and Verdel called me into a private room. He told me that God had been waking him up in the middle of the night for several nights with a Word for me. Verdel spoke clearly to me, saying God

said "that if I would seek Him first, then my family would follow." Verdel went on to tell me that he had to be obedient and give me this information from God because it was critical. Verdel delivered the message from God with such fire and urgency, but compassion and love. I knew Verdel had a close walk with the Lord and did not have any doubt that God gave the message to Verdel because I wasn't listening. Verdel did not know that I had been in a hot and cold relationship with God for some years. Prior to working with Verdel, I had attended Bible College and ministry at different times, so I knew exactly what God's message through Verdel meant.

I grabbed that word from God with the same fire that Verdel delivered it, and followed it up with a period of time seeking God through His Word in the morning and prayer. As I began to truly seek God, my family followed, just like God said. This was a very spiritually enriching time for me and my family. We had a son that was having some serious problems and I knew Verdel was praying for him as well. However, after I began seeking God, God began to move in my son's life, just as Verdel said he would do. My son drew closer to God, as I would send text messages that included scripture verses to my son and he would say how he loved them and to keep sending them. My entire family became closer to Jesus because of Verdel. Not everybody would approach a friend with a message from God like Verdel did, but I am eternally grateful for Verdel, his friendship and his obedience to God.

So, there you go. I married an amazing man, the same man who raised Jon and Kait. I went to church the day after Verdel's service and two young men spoke to me. They expressed how moved they were by the service and how Verdel's life had inspired them to become better husbands, fathers, and people.

"To God be the glory," was all I could say. I was still in shock and disbelief, and my emotions were hard to describe.

Weeks later high school and college friends of mine that had never met my husband or only had a brief encounter with him at reunions or other festivities, texted, sent cards, even wrote letters that they were so moved by Verdel's impact that they wanted to re-dedicate their life to God, be better for their family, and find their purpose. Again, my response was the same, "to God be all the glory and what a blessing." It had been an honor to be Verdel's wife, and now it is an honor to be his widow. There was no end to the number of people who talked about how much Verdel changed their lives.

Impact can be defined as a forceful collision of one thing with another or as a powerful or significant influence or effect. People from all walks of life — family, friends, church members, coaches, teachers, co-workers, spouses, and even Facebook friends — talked about the impact Verdel had on their lives, whether it was through personal interaction or by attending his victory celebration. People shared encounters, memories, conversations, or encouragement they received from him that impacted them profoundly, unforgettably positively and blessedly. I'm sure you're reading this and thinking, "Oh, what a blessing for them."

But let me tell you what I was doing at the time. I was doing everything in my power to make sure Verdel's death didn't destroy me or my kids, physically and mentally. We were dealing with depression, anxiety, isolation, and thoughts of suicide. I felt as if we were drowning in sadness. I had no plan for this nor did I plan for it. Who plans to become a widow anyway?

I remember when Bishop Heron Johnson married us; our vow was till death do us part. I had only focused on living. Because I walked in faith, I never entertained thoughts of death because I believed God would heal Verdel. Please understand and know I still believe God! It is clear to me that God can do anything, and I am learning to live by His sovereign will. God chose to heal Verdel through death and that's part of God's sovereignty. Revelations 14:13 (KJV), reads, *"And I heard a voice from heaven saying unto me, Write, Blessed are the dead which die in the Lord from henceforth: Yea, saith the Spirit, that they may rest from the labour; and their works do follow them."*

Verdel's passing had devastating affect not just for me and our children, but our family, friends, church, and his co-workers. When Verdel's team was told that he had passed, one man literally bolted out of the door, down the stairs, and into the middle of the street screaming. As soon as they got him out of the street, he was taken home. Dear friends who were regulars at our home would now have trouble coming over. They would sit in the driveway and cry. Whenever I tried to talk to someone about my feelings, I ended up comforting them instead. Everyone seemed to be just as devastated as Jon, Kait, and me.

Weeping, I thought how heartbroken Verdel would be to see us in such pain and despair because of his death. I knew he wouldn't want us to stay in mourning for too long. However, grief felt so heavy, like a boulder I couldn't carry. My grief was like a heavy cape that made every move, thought, and act hard.

It was easier to sleep. The kids told me that I was "moping" around. That's what TeamMartin calls it when someone is walking around looking sad and lost, unable get their act together.

During a drive home one evening, the three of us started talking about Verdel as we entered the neighborhood. Jon said, "Mom you're moping. I know you miss him. Maybe if you think about your dates and the trips it will help you. We think of good things and it helps us."

I guess therapy was *working* for them. Jon and Kait had typical challenges of teenagers — school, friends, frenemies, and social media. All three of us went to therapy, and grief counseling. We went together and separately. Again, I still believe God and I believe that therapy, counseling and professional services can provide great benefits for those dealing with grief.

One afternoon on the way from therapy, I asked Kait what did they do during her session. She told me about the exercise she'd done. She was given a sheet of paper with a figure on it and asked to color any place that was hurt or made her sad because of her dad's death. Kait said, "Sometimes my stomach hurts, so I colored my tummy."

"Okay. Where else did you color?" I asked. It was a presumptuous question.

"That's it," Kait said.

"You sure?" I asked.

"Yes," she said.

"So not your heart or your head?" I said.

"No ma'am," she said. "God has a plan. I don't know what it is, but I know He has a plan."

I almost ran off the road because I turned around to look at my daughter. She was clearly trusting God more than I did at the moment. Her words left me fighting back tears and fighting to stay on the roadway.

"Okay, Kait. We're going to trust God's plan for us."

In a strange way, the reminder to trust God led me back to the word impact. The impact of Verdel's death seemed to be all consuming, overshadowing, and obscuring the beauty of his life until then. But God allowed me to reflect on Verdel's life, Verdel's courage, Verdel's faith, Verdel's walk with God, Verdel's love for his family — biological and extended, his love for his Sunday Schools students, and the love he had for his colleagues. Verdel's life mattered so much, and so much had been shared and said by his life. I told God that I would not allow Verdel's death to have greater impact than his life. In his life, Verdel served others, loved his family and was a good example for others. Even if it were just for me, Jon and Kait, death was no longer stealing the spotlight and we would not be casualties of grief.

Was it easy? Absolutely not. We made intentional choices like celebrating Verdel's birthday. Yes, we can observe his passing and gather for support and comfort, but we choose to celebrate his life and those he touched. We remembered, journaled, talked, laughed, and tried to recreate past events. We laughed when we failed and cheered when we got it right. We learned what we could handle on our own and when it was time to call in the experts like the repair person.

About a year after Verdel passed, the garbage disposal stopped working. For a solid week, I tried to fix it. I watched countless YouTube videos, donned gloves and used Verdel's tools to attempt the repair. I gave it my all, but I couldn't fix it. The kitchen sink was clogged and the stench was unbearable. My children finally said, "Mom, you're not Dad. You are Mom. It's ok. But please call somebody it stinks in here!"

That incident and my therapist taught me that I had three buckets available to me at all times: NOW, LATER and DELEGATE. These buckets helped us process and plan life, while avoiding being overwhelmed and feeling a frantic panic. These buckets helped us move forward. As we learned to use our buckets wisely, we learned to live again. We began to smile, we found joy, and we stepped out of the cave of despair. We pulled down the gloomy curtains of grief that shrouded our lives.

I believe these figurative buckets can help you move forward in your journey to joy. Whether you make physical, electronic, or mental notes, using these buckets will bring clarity and calmness to the daily challenges of life.

There are moments Jon and Kait will say, "What would Dad say?" Sometimes they asked me, sometimes I asked them. Kait recently said, "Mom, I'm not sure what Dad would say about…" I said, "I don't know either Rock Star, but God has given you people who love you, share our values, and offer you the same godly wisdom, and counsel as your father." I thank God for these men: Pastor Gerry Bivins, Prothaniel Harris, and John Brown.

Occasionally, I even think to myself, "What would Verdel do, think or say about this? What would his strategy be?" I'd tell myself, "Verdel would ask God." Because I've found his methods to be wise and sound, I sometimes resolve things the way Verdel would. There are other things I approach like Robbie, embracing my own capacity. But whether I lean toward Robbie or Verdel, I want God's guidance.

The impact of Verdel's death took us through many trials and left us with some scars, but I believe we're on the other side now. Our scars have given us character, compassion, wisdom, and strength. They remind us that we fought a battle, but we were victorious. Our scars serve as a testament to help others heal. Scars are also the price for love, and we wouldn't trade that love for anything. So having learned about the effect of impact, I challenge you:

Don't let your loved one's death impact you more than their life. Remember them, celebrate them, and know their desire for you is to be happy and to live in joy.

STEELE MARTIN

5 | Mind Your Business, Please

No one gets to tell you that "you should be over that by now." It's what I call "compounded grief." You are already experiencing day-to-day grief and someone adds to grief with comments about what you are or are not processing and moving forward, thus compounding your grief. Have you ever been on the receiving end of comments like, "Aren't you over that yet?" Or "Okay, darling it's time to let that go." It's time to move on, or the classic, "You can't stay like that forever."

These words, perhaps well-intentioned, often come with a flawed approach. Grief makes people uncomfortable. Grief is not really something people want to talk about, but because we have been raised in a society where it's polite to ask "how are you doing?" We have been conditioned to say "I'm praying for you." But, let's be honest, most people do not want to hear how you are dealing with grief because that discomfort disturbs their emotional space, adds to it, or makes their own pain worse. Because of this, their communication to people experiencing grief is often not well thought out and completely inconsiderate. Many people may be concerned about how your situation will affect their already overflowing and unstable emotional state, or they can be thankful that they have reached a place of joy and peace, so adding your issues upsets their applecart. As a result, we may hear phrases like "let's move on," "don't stay like," and "that this too shall pass." For some, that's all they can manage and that's okay. However, for those of us experiencing grief, our authentic internal response is "why would you ask me if you didn't want to hear me?" or "you should have kept that to yourself," while our polite external response is "Thanks" as we gracefully exit the conversation.

After Verdel's death, I was asked when the kids and I were moving out of our family home. This insensitive person assumed that we had to move or that we wanted to move. Neither was true. A few months into widowhood, I was shocked by this question while feeling vulnerable and unstable. I was grateful that I was able to respond, "Verdel took care of everything" and quickly walked away as tears began to fall. I was also grateful my kids weren't around for that interaction.

Another well meaning, but insensitive question is the all-time "what happened?" This is a question that many of us receive when our loved ones die. My take on this question and any response, if someone wants you to know those details, they will share unprompted. Otherwise, the fact of death is not changed by knowledge of circumstances surrounding the death. The fact that a grieving family needs prayer and support is paramount. So, whether you choose to answer the question at all and how you choose to answer it is up to you. Outside of children, immediate family and, maybe, inner-circle, you don't owe anyone any extended details. Also, as you breathe through the processing moments of these questions, you gain clarity on how to respond.

I vividly remember an incident at the hair salon several years before the pandemic. The hair salon, as you know, is not just a place for self-care, but also a social hub. In my stylist's room, alongside her styling chair, were chairs for waiting clients. I was seated in one, awaiting my standing Thursday night appointment while engaged in conversation with my stylist about my father's upcoming wedding. My parents were married thirty-five years before my mother passed in 1998. It was a union that weathered job losses, layoffs, my mother's battle with breast cancer, and my father's drug use before he gave his life to Christ. Their love was unwavering.

After my mother's passing, my father was left devastated, and for a while, it seemed as though he was losing his grip on reality. His behavior became erratic, unpredictable, and his grief was raw, unapologetic, extreme, and at times, downright ugly. It wasn't until I experienced the loss of my own spouse that I revisited his actions and realized that he was doing his best to navigate the waters of grief, armed only with the resources available to him. My father didn't receive any individualized grief counseling following my mother's death; he did attend a few group sessions for recently widowed individuals, but it only lasted six months. As for individual counseling, I'm uncertain whether he didn't want it, didn't think about it, or know if that type of grief counseling was available for him.

Fast forward to 2001, and my father is engaged to be married. My mother's death in 1998, at the age of 54, left me shattered. In 1999, I had married the love of my life, and my mother wasn't there to celebrate with us. Now my father was preparing to remarry and I was pregnant with my first child. My mother's absence loomed heavily. It felt like I was on a never-ending emotional roller coaster ride. So, there I sat in the salon, pouring out my feelings to my stylist. Our conversation naturally drifted towards my mother's passing and how we were all, including my stylist, processing the loss of someone who had been a blessing to so many.

You see, I believe that anyone fulfilling their God-given purpose is indeed a blessing to us all. Our conversation shifted to my personal journey of processing my mother's death, including triggers. My mother passed before I got married, so she did not help me select my wedding dress, the right flowers, or to fuss about invitations. She wasn't there to attend any obstetrician appointments or shopping for baby clothes either. As I grappled with these emotions, I confessed, "I don't really know what to call her. I'm not comfortable calling her by her first name, I just don't think that's appropriate." After I said this, another customer, who I had not been talking to, inserted herself into our conversation, and said "Girl, you should be over that by now. If she's marrying your daddy, then you call her mama."

A stunned silence descended upon the room, and I felt as if I were on one of those television shows, where people's heads swivel back and forth between two conversationalists, much like a tennis match. Suddenly, I felt like I was seeing flashes of light, probably because my blood pressure was rising. Completely forgetting about my stylist, me, my emotions, and my pregnant belly got out of that chair, walked across the room to the woman, and leaned over, and with a steely voice asked her "Is your mother still alive?" Taken aback, she stammered, "Yes, you know she is." I said "Then how in the world are you going to tell me that I should be over my mother's death? You have never walked in my shoes. You still have your mom. I didn't ask you your opinion, so I suggest you shut up and sit quietly until it's your turn. Do not say anything else to me." With that, me, my emotions and pregnant belly returned to the stylist's chair.

As you absorb my behavior during this incident, let's break down what transpired:

1. **Mind Your Surroundings.** I was discussing an emotional and sensitive issue openly where others could hear and chime in. Lesson learned! I was having a conversation with my stylist as if we were the only people in the room. Possibly because I chose to continue my personal conversation in an open area, others felt it was okay to join in and comment.

2. **Seek to Understand.** Even though I knew her mother was alive, I did not know anything about her family, upbringing, or dynamics. To me, the title "Mom and Dad" implies reverence, respect, love, and a significant relationship. However, some people grow up calling their friends' parents mama or daddy, so for them mama and daddy are defined by roles rather than by relationship.

3. **Protect Your Heart.** The moment my brain processed her comment, I knew I was about to lose it. Her addition

to the conversation did not create positive or helpful impression. It was up to me to protect my fragile heart and headspace at that moment. You should not be afraid to end conversations online or in person, or to remove yourself from toxic conversations or interactions.

Below are some conversation strategies for your journey to joy.

1.**Breathe Through It:** Take a moment to just breathe. Take several full deep cleansing breaths. As you exhale, push the awkward, toxic, or inappropriate comment out of your mind. As you inhale, concentrate on something that brings you joy. Breathing and replacing thoughts will help you regain and maintain your center.

2. **Extend Grace to Ourselves:** Comments like "get over it," "move on," "still holding on," or "you haven't processed that yet" can cut deep for those experiencing grief. Our reality is that we don't want to endure this ordeal. We long to restore our loved one to their place in the world. We yearn to mend our shattered lives, end the relentless pain, and escape the uninvited agony. Our lives have been fractured, and we're navigating the complex terrain of grief. However, we must remind ourselves that processing grief is part of the journey and everyone doesn't move through the journey at the same speed. We must extend grace for the journey, even when others do not.

3. **Support Comes from God:** Whenever someone asks how we're doing or inserts themselves into our journey, it's essential to set realistic expectations. Our ultimate source of

support comes from God. For me, God has been specific in who he has sent to me and my children. Moreover, God has given me an ear to hear what is being said. As you pray, ask God to let your ears be so sensitive and discerning that you can sense when something is coming from Him, or what I refer to as "just chatter that does not matter." If you move in this direction, you realize God's words, messages, and encouragement is specifically designed for you in this season and the ones He is directing toward you.

4. **Guarding Yourself and Your Family is Paramount.** Some people are merely curious or nosy, seeking to satisfy their idle curiosity. They bombard you with uncomfortable questions, showing more interest in the drama than your well-being. Then there are the professional mourners. You know those who cry on cue, often more than you do. These attention-seekers should be avoided as their insensitive antics can be triggering. Being open doesn't mean letting just anyone into your life during times of grief. The act of guarding is essential, ensuring that only those who genuinely offer support and solace are allowed in. You and your family should avoid these people because their ill-conceived attempts to gain attention can be unnecessary triggers.

5. **Be Open to Hear Who God Sends:** Remember, you don't know everything! We have finite minds. There is a limit to our understanding. Most of us don't even use the our brains to the fullest extent. This is particularly relevant during times of grief and loss.

In the middle of writing this chapter at my kitchen table, someone from Washington, DC contacted me. The message came through Facebook: *"Hey, beautiful friend just doing a quick check to see if you're okay and to say I love you. Maybe I'm silly, but I just felt like reaching out."*

The text took me straight into worship, if you know me, then you understand! I live in Hoover, Alabama and Wendy Jackson lives in DC. We haven't spoken in over two years. But that day, as I wrote about being open to who God sends, she texted me to encourage me, to tell me to keep going. What a beautiful God moment of confirmation.

> *"Aww, my beautiful friend. God sent you right on time. Continue to pray for me. I am pushing through a project that's emotionally challenging, but I'm making it," I responded back. "Thank you, and I love you."*

> *"I love you, too," Wendy wrote. "I am praying and know God and you got this! (Emojis praying and hearts.) Let me know if I can help."*

> *"Wendy! You have no idea how you just helped me. I'm literally wowed at God," I wrote back. "I am writing a book about grief to joy. The chapter that I am writing right now is about being open to who God sends to encourage or help you, even if they don't look like who you are expecting. Then you texted me. God just confirmed that I am writing what He wants. I am in awe. I love you and thank you for being obedient."*

> *"Oh wow! I saw it in your eyes in one of your Facebook photos. I felt His voice saying Robbie needs to hear from you," Wendy wrote. "Some days I don't feel worthy, but perhaps He is using your need to remind me that God can*

use us. I hope your book is a bestseller. Many people are grieving. What a help it will be to many. You got this!"

"Thank you so much. This is so on time, and I receive that in Jesus' name," I texted. *"It will bless many. Bestseller in Jesus name."*

"Amen!" Wendy wrote.

In conclusion, Wendy and I couldn't be more different — different races, generations, and geographic locations. Yet, her timely text message was a powerful reminder of how God uses whomever He chooses. God is trustworthy and worthy of our confidence. We must embrace those He sends to help, bless, support, and encourage us. They are on a divine assignment, and the delivery is their responsibility, while acceptance is ours.

If we don't listen to God's leading, we can miss the people God is sending to inspire, strengthen, and comfort us. Like the lady in the grocery store who walked up to me with an encouraging message, or the acquaintance who sent a timely text. Their familiarity or lack thereof doesn't matter. What they say or do confirms something God has already spoken to you. These individuals are on assignment, and you are their assignment. Embrace their presence and their words, recognizing that God works through mysterious and unexpected channels. God's help isn't limited by our finite minds or preconceived notions. It is our responsibility to accept those whom God sends our way. Remember, we don't know everything, and God can use anyone to bring comfort and strength.

Let's pause here to discuss what it means to be "open." When you are grieving and coping with loss, being open does not mean that everyone can enter your space. My opinion is that this principle applies throughout your life, but especially during times of grief and loss. Protection for oneself and for one's family is crucial, as we discussed before. Let's face it, some people are just nosey. Some people just want to know what happened, how you're doing, how you're feeling, who was there, what they did, did she cry, and how they looked. These people aren't from God, you know that. If you find yourself bombarded with uncomfortable questions and you never feel uplifted and strengthened, that is not the one for you. You don't have to deal with them. It's not necessary for you to answer questions, calls, or texts. I'm also talking about the professional mourners who come already red-eyed and crying on cue. God did not send these attention seekers either to assist you on your journey from grief to joy.

Open means I may be conversing with someone unfamiliar to me or unfamiliar to me in the light I am seeing them, but what they say/do confirms something God has already revealed. As Holy Spirit connects what this person says or does with me, I know it is God who is at work. You know that lady in the grocery store who says, "I'm just being obedient and God told me to tell you that He is with you and He heard your prayer." Those are real God-appointed encounters.

Have you ever questioned the timing of a text message? During a period of intense grieving, when you are feeling overwhelmed by pain and thinking you're about to collapse?

You receive a text message or call that uplifts and shifts you out of pain. The next time you get a text from someone you don't really talk to very often, the message could be short and straight to the point, "God is with you, hold on sis." Or the text could be a scripture to encourage you. Those people don't really know you, but they're on assignment. It could also be your best friend or someone you have a strong connection with whose assignments are much easier to understand and embrace. We often struggle to accept those we don't understand or recognize. In the end, we must remember that our help comes from God and He chooses when and who He wants to use. It's our job to accept who God sends.

Remember, we don't know everything. It is impossible for us to know what God has brought others through, or what revelations He has given them. Don't rely on what your natural eyes see. Do not place your acceptance in the hand of the person who you believe will fulfill your expectations of your help. God's movement, God's plan, God's blessing, and God's help during a time of loss and grief are beyond comprehension. We serve the great God of glory, who can spring up a pool of water in the desert for us to drink.

> *"I will open rivers in high places, and fountains in the midst of the valleys: I will make the wilderness a pool of water, and the dry land springs of water. I will plant in the wilderness the cedar, the shittah tree, and the myrtle, and the oil tree; I will set in the desert the fir tree, and the pine, and the box tree together." Isaiah 41:18-19 (KJV).*

God doesn't need or require us to approve of those He sends to encourage us. Accepting those sent to help us increases our faith and shows our reliance on God. Accept the help, blessing, support, and encouragement God sends your way. They are on assignment, and so you are. The delivery is theirs, the acceptance is yours.

6 | Grace to Grieve

Grief is a relentless, unforgiving, and uncomfortable emotion. It weaves its way into the very fabric of your being, leaving no aspect of your life untouched. It thrusts the person experiencing it into an uncomfortable, suffocating embrace, and its presence creates a palpable discomfort for anyone who dares to engage with the affected soul. Nobody willingly signs up for the anguish grief brings. I've often yearned to convey to those who visibly squirm in my presence as a new widow.

Guess what? Their discomfort, as real as it is, but a fleeting moment for them. It's a temporary discomfort. For us, though, grief is a constant companion. It greets me in the morning, linger throughout the day, and tucks me in at night. I share my meals with grief, do life alongside it, and, believe it or not, even find moments of laughter colored by its presence. Grief, you see, wears many faces. It can be soft as cotton with quiet tears, or as sharp as blade with tears that thunder our hearts and quake our bodies. We can appear composed, articulate and well put together the surface, yet inside, we're falling apart.

What I'm trying to convey is this: grief demands grace. Earlier, we defined grief as the price we pay when a loved one dies. Grief necessitates grace — grace for the space, grace for the journey, grace for what lies ahead, grace for what you are going to learn about yourself and grace for what God will reveal to you.

Around two weeks before Kait graduated high school, marking almost six years into widowhood, I started having these intense sobbing episodes and crying multiple times a day. The onset of these episodes was nothing short of a tempest. They seemed to manifest out of thin air and the frequency was too numerous to count. Tears flowed unabated staining every corner of my life — in the car, in the office, in the store, during meetings, and even while sharing a simple lunch with friends. I attempted to dissect the triggers for these sudden, intense waves of sorrow. God had been faithfully walking with me through the pain of loss. I felt like I had made some strides in my journey. Life was finally beginning to shine with glimmers of joy, which made this sobbing episodes more unnerving. I felt like I was spiraling out of control, as though I had no mastery over my own emotions.

The tears were determined, it seemed, to wash away all the evidence of God's faithfulness during my widowhood. They threatened to erase the wisdom and coping strategies I had acquired through therapy. It was as if I had been hurled back into the inky abyss of grief's earliest days when makeup was an impractical accessory since it would invariably be wiped away by the constant cascade of tears. These were not the gentle, dignified tears that slid gracefully down one's cheeks. No. These were torrents, bursting forth with such intensity that they leapt from my eyes, drenching clothes and spilling onto my lap. They streamed down my face, escaping through the sides of my eyes. My nose ran and sobs choked my words. This was grief in its most unfiltered, visceral form returning and I was freaking out.

And to exacerbate matters, insomnia returned. I wrestled with it during the early days of my widowhood. Insomnia is an all-too-familiar companion for those navigating grief, for a number of reasons. While the mind is reeling in shock, struggles to process this life event, the body is completely out of whack, nerves are heightened, headaches may manifest, as do physical pain and digestive issues. Eating becomes a burdensome chore or constant solace, and life's comforting routines vanish into thin air.

Sleep becomes an elusive luxury when you've lost a spouse. The absence of your partner in the most intimate space in your home, once your sanctuary for love, intimacy, and shared moments — tender and trivial — now looms like a cavernous void in your home, your bedroom, and your bed. The space where two hearts beat in harmony, where laughter and love thrived now feels cold and desolate. The space where two became one, and now the one is alone.

I tried everything, but nothing seemed to work. I tried it all —— changing rooms, altering colors, redecorating, and even replacing the bedding. I attempted to metamorphose the space into something distinctly mine. Yet, not one thing seemed to work. I wandered through life like a sleep-deprived zombie, collapsing on the couch, the chaise, the floor, or my children's beds when I spent time with them. I yearned for the rest I so desperately needed, but it seemed out of reach. I know God is my source of rest and stillness, as scripture teaches in Matthew 11:28-30 (KJV): *"Come unto me, all ye that labour and are heavy laden, and I will give you rest. Take my yoke upon you, and learn of me; for I am meek and lowly in heart: and ye shall find rest unto your souls. For my yoke is easy, and my burden is light."*

When I could muster the strength to pray, my pleas were sobs. Sometimes, no words came from my trembling lips, only tears. I felt akin to Hannah in 1 Samuel 1:10-17. Tears and sobs were my language to God. But God, in His boundless compassion, comprehended my pain, as evidenced by my tear-stained prayers and my inability to articulate the anguish within. In the midst of my agony, God provided me with a specific path to vanquish insomnia. He revealed to me that just as Verdel and I had become one during our years of marriage, I needed some godly couples who shared that profound oneness to pray for me concerning this specific area. Without hesitation, and driven by sheer desperation, I approached my then pastor and his wife, my godparents, and to our dearest friends, the Harrises, the Augusts, the Carews, the Bivins, the Browns and the Bumpuses. I implored these couples to pray fervently for me, my children, our home, and the return of rest. And let me tell you, in less than a week my insomnia dissipated without the need for medication or external intervention. God had once again displayed His unwavering faithfulness, and I had no intentions of relinquishing the victory He bestowed upon me.

The resurgence of sobbing and insomnia led me to believe that I had regressed in my journey of healing. I was consumed by deep-seated concerns, my heart weighed down by sorrow, and frankly, I stood on the precipice of a meltdown.

What had I done wrong? I attempted to grapple with it alone, neglecting to seek God's counsel. I failed to inquire of God, to ask Him why, what, and how. Panic set in, as I feared my newfound normalcy would be supplanted by an unending cycle of misery. I endeavored to diagnose my condition myself, convinced that the return of my sobbing and insomnia was an unequivocal sign that I had retraced my steps to the starting point of my recovery journey. But, I was wrong.

In this season of my journey, I learned, slowly but surely, to extend grace to myself, and to cease judging myself for not perpetually moving forward, for moments of feeling stuck, and even for periods of regression. It was unreasonable to expect my emotions to follow a linear trajectory. After all, I had shared seventeen profound years with an extraordinary man. Some days the pain was piercing, and I longed for his presence. I wanted my husband back and I wanted my life back in tact. These were rational emotions, and they shouldn't be dismissed on the grounds of an arbitrary timeline. I allowed myself the freedom to grieve, to cry, to feel, and to continue healing. I acknowledged that tears were not indicative of stagnation. They were part and parcel of my ongoing journey.

Tears did not signify regression. There were simply another peak in the jagged landscape of my journey. I kept climbing because God equipped me with hind feet. *"The Lord God is my strength, and he will make my feet like hinds' feet, and he will make me to walk upon mine high places." Habakkuk 3:19* (KJV)

My Grandmother Flora reminded me that grief is as slippery as okra. It strives to drag us back, to erode the progress we've painstakingly made. But, progress is not always measured in a linear fashion. Sometimes it is counted in months, weeks, days, or even hours. Some days you might inch forward second-by-second. Wherever you find yourself on your journey, whether you're struggling to take a single step, or making great strides, remember this: tears are not a sign of regression. Tears are both the process and the progress. So, grant yourself the grace to grieve.

What does it mean to give yourself grace as you navigate the turbulent seas of grief?

1. **Talk to God About It**. Pray about everything. Even your tears. Seeking God in all matters is a powerful testament to your unwavering trust in God. As you may have experienced, God listens, understands, and provides clarity, peace, and answers in His own way and time.
2. **Don't Judge Yourself.** It's natural to be your harshest critic when you are grieving. In the times you find yourself judging your own progress because of the tears, it's crucial to remind yourself that healing isn't a linear journey. It's a winding path with peaks and valleys, and sometimes, those tears are simply a part of the terrain.
3. **Set Realistic Expectations.** Grief is the cost of love. Expecting yourself to turn off your grief like a light switch is unrealistic. Instead, it's about acknowledging the reality of your pain and allowing yourself to experience it in all its

rawness. By doing so, you're not just mourning loss, you're also celebrating the love that once filled your life.

4. **Resist External Definitions.** Others may try to define your recover journey for you, imposing their timelines and expectations. Do not allow friends, family, or co-workers to dictate your pace. Grief is deeply personal and your journey is uniquely your own.

5. **Journal Your Thoughts.** Keep a journal, not just of your feelings and thoughts, but also of your moods, actions, reactions, trends, and patterns. This practice will help you identify triggers that might not be immediately apparent, empowering you to navigate your journey to joy.

6. **Allow Space and Time.** Allowing yourself the space and time to cry or grieve is vital. In my recovery journey, I learned to allow myself to feel whatever sadness, reflect on memories, or simply endure a tough day. These moments often pave the way for significant steps forward in your journey to joy.

Give yourself grace to cry, feel, and heal. Your tears are not indicators of regressions, they are sign posts on your journey. Your love was deep and profound, and your grief is the price you pay for that love. It's a process, a progression, and sometimes it's inching forward second-by-second. You'll learn that although grief is as slippery as okra — ever trying to pull you back — keep climbing, propelled by God's grace, understanding that grief is as slippery as okra, ever trying to pull you back. Give yourself the grace to grieve no matter how long, how messy or how many tears you cry. You are on your own time clock.

7 | Triggers, Unwelcome Visitors

Triggers, those unwelcome companions of grief, can be like sudden thunderstorms that strike without warning. They're unexpected waves that toss you back into grief's tempest. They materialize in various forms, both anticipated and out of the blue.

My definition of grief triggers is "experiences that bring about powerful feelings and emotional responses when reminded of the death of a loved one." It can be anything that triggers you to revert back to grief without warning. Often, triggers are unexpected accounts with some stimulus (optical or otherwise) that can transport your mind (and sometimes your body) back to specific moment of loss or grief. Some other triggers may include dates and milestones, anniversaries, special occasions, unique places, photographs, favorite sayings, and smells.

In the aftermath of Verdel's death, I recall returning to work after taking an extended leave. I was the only woman in a meeting about scheduled maintenance on some building machinery. I was fine with that, since it was not uncommon in my position. The gentleman's phone next to me started ringing while we were in the meeting. Suddenly, I became unglued. I imagine it was how Wiley Coyote felt every time Road Runner sped past him detaching his body parts. As the phone rang, my heart dropped. I had that very ringtone assigned to Verdel. It was a very unique ringtone. I actually stood up and reached for this man's phone. Then I realized everyone was watching me. I stood there speechless, tears jumping out of my eyes clutching a phone that wasn't even mine.

I gave the man his phone, picked up my notebook, my phone and exited without a word of explanation. That was one of the worst triggers I ever experienced.

On another occasion, I received a call as I was rushing to catch an elevator for an in-person meeting. As the elevator doors opened, there was something about the smell of the elevator, coupled with my rush to get on the elevator — the same elevator I rushed to get on the day I left my office to get to the hospital for my beloved Verdel. Although I was physically headed to the meeting, mentally and emotionally I was back in critical care unit with my husband watching doctors and nurses move around me. I saw myself praying and crying as a nurse moved me out of the room.

I was reliving the moments of my husband's transition. Physically, I had backed into the corner of the elevator. I don't know how long I stood in there. I never made it to my meeting. Finally, I ran out of the building and to the parking lot. I was unable to think or function. I had lost time and awareness. This was a devastating and alarm trigger experience.

If triggers threaten to hold you captive, remember this: some triggers are identifiable, like dates, events, anniversaries, birthdays, holidays, and locations. Triggers can be anticipated and managed, even in the age of social media, if you have a strategy.

Here are my trigger strategies. I hope they help you navigate your triggers:

Strategy 1. **Be Friends with a Calendar:** Know what's coming up, anticipate triggers, and develop a response plan.

Strategy 2. **Anticipate Location Triggers:** Have alternate routes and options in mind.

Strategy 3. **Establish Safe Spaces:** Identify places where you can find solace and regain composure.

Strategy 4. **Affirm the Present:** Remind yourself of the current moment with a positive affirmation.

Strategy 5. **Recognize the Trigger:** Acknowledge it for what it is as a trigger—and don't let it derail your journey.

Around my third year of widowhood, I started understanding my triggers better. God equipped me with wisdom, strength, and strategies to manage them. On holidays like Valentine's Day, Mother's Day, and Father's Day, I steer clear of social media for the day, sometimes even for a few days. This is depending on my mood. I might post something to honor my parents or my beloved if I feel up to it, but I consciously avoid scrolling through posts of love and admiration for spouses. I cherish those posts, but they often trigger my grief.

Avoiding social media on trigger days is entirely acceptable. This is just as it's perfectly fine to bypass the cologne counter in a department store if a particular scent triggers your emotions. You don't have to avoid the entire mall; instead, take an alternate route. Don't let the trigger win. You can do it. Remember Philippians 4:11-13 (KJV) says, *"Not that I speak in respect of want: for I have learned, in whatsoever state I am, therewith to be content. I know both how to be abased, and I know how to abound: every where and in all things I am instructed both to be full and to be hungry, both to abound and to suffer need. I can do all things through Christ which strengtheneth me."*

I've found that recognizing triggers, staying calm, and reminding myself of the present with affirmations are powerful strategies. By meditating on God's word and focusing on a series of tasks, I've shifted my mind away from triggers. I believe you can too.

Thank God for the strength and strategies to recognize and manage triggers. We may never fully eliminate them, but we can navigate them with wisdom, faith, and perseverance.

"For God hath not given us the spirit of fear; but of power, and of love, and of a sound mind." 2 Timothy 1:7 (KJV)

"Blessed be God, even the Father of our Lord Jesus Christ, the Father of mercies, and the God of all comfort; Who comforteth us in all our tribulation, that we may be able to comfort them which are in any trouble, by the comfort wherewith we ourselves are comforted of God. For as the

sufferings of Christ abound in us, so our consolation also aboundeth by Christ. 2 Corinthians1:3-5 (KJV)

STEELE MARTIN

8 | Dancing in the Rain

Verdel passed on Monday, October 10, 2016. For about two years after his death, Mondays and the 10th of any month were triggers for me. On Saturday, I would begin to dread Monday. Then, from Sunday to Tuesday, I would experience what I called a "frantic panic" — inability to concentrate, constantly losing track of time and losing items. Verdel's death was associated with those dates and days in my mind and heart.

During my recovery journey, I have learned that triggers can take both expected and unexpected forms. My recovery has also been boosted by God's wisdom in recognizing triggers, establishing a plan of action, and managing triggers in a way that does not hinder my progress.

It has been seven years since I began my recovery journey. I've managed (this does not mean I don't have them at all, this means when I do have them I can get through them and over them without feeling derailed) using God's strategies. Unexpected triggers have proven more challenging. One moment we can be fine, and the next, life triggers feelings of sadness, pain, and anger.

When my grief met my God, my grief had to bow! God almighty is our creator. He alone is God. Nothing, including grief is greater! By faith in Jesus Christ, we are more than conquerors, so we can overcome grief and sorrow. Jesus is our victor, not our own power, light, or strength.

Unexpected triggers are elusive and cannot be predicted or scheduled. They do not play fair. Often, they have the audacity to be accompanied by other difficult, painful, hurtful, crisis-ridden situations, and circumstances along with them, such as the experience I'm sharing.

One Sunday morning, I left home headed to church. Halfway through my forty-minute commute, I noticed that my tire air pressure light was illuminated. As I pulled into the service station near the air pump it started to rain. Attaching the air pump to the tire, I said to myself, "fine, no big deal, I got this." I told myself I'd get the tire pressure up and still make it to church on time. Back in the car, I checked the air pressure, but nothing had changed. With me, operator error is always a possibility, so I started the process of positive thinking. I still have time, it's just sprinkling. Once again, I checked the tire's air pressure, still no change. I begin to consider that maybe the pump is not working. So, I drive further down the road to the next gas station. As I pull into the gas station, the rain goes from light sprinkle to downpour.

I keep telling myself, you got this. As soon as I see a break in the rain, I'll get out of the car and purchase time on the air pump. The pump revs up. A quick check of the tire indicator on my dash shows that the pressure has dropped from twenty-four to fourteen. I could actually see the tire going flat. Tears streamed down my face with the rain. I sat there remembering that I was a widow with no one to call. No one was coming to my rescue. My hero, the man who cared how my day went, that I was safe, if my car had gas and all of my tires were good had been snatched from me.

    Because of the rain, no one at the gas station realized I was crying or that I needed assistance. No one stopped. I was crying. The sky was crying. I was triggered by a stupid flat tire. I closed my eyes, wishing myself back home in bed with my weighted blanket over my head. I opened my eyes, I was still in the car. I closed my eyes again. This time there were images of Verdel saying "hurry up, we're gonna be late for Sunday School." I wanted to stay in that moment riding to church listening to Verdel talking about the Sunday School lesson while the kids were laughing and making jokes. I took a long, deep breath with my eyes still closed absorbing all the joy this vision allowed. I opened my eyes. I was still sitting in my car with a flat tire in the rain. I took another deep breath, realizing I had been triggered. I forced my brain into strategy mode: Strategy No. 3, be in a safe space. Strategy No. 5, remind yourself to stay positive, Robbie. You are not alone. Jesus is right here. He is your present help.

    As I talked to myself, the tears subsided, but the rain came down harder. Strategy No. 4, be in the present. "Okay, Lord, what am I going to do? This tire is low." Ding, Ding, Ding! I had a light bulb moment: I was headed to church. Calling the church seem like a logical idea, and would not require much cerebral prowess. In my haste, (but God's plan), I call my Pastor instead of the church. He answered the phone on the first ring and said, "My wife just asked me about you. I was looking for you earlier. Are you okay?" I melted into a puddle. In two sentences my Pastor shut down the dark, grief-weighted thoughts that I was alone, and no one cared about me.

At that moment, I didn't even try to fight back the tears, I cried. "No, I'm not okay. I've got a flat and I'm stuck sitting here in the rain." My pastor asked where I was and if I was safe. I just kept crying trying to explain that I was about fifteen minutes away from the church. "Robbie, it's okay" was all I heard as rain pounded on the roof of the car, the windshield, and the hood. It felt as though the rain was pounding on my head and tears streamed down my face.

"Can you drive any further?" asked my Pastor.

"I don't know. I'm scared. The tire is so flat," I said.

"Go very slow. I'll stay on the phone with you," he said.

I drove about five minutes when the car started making a loud, alarming sound. More tears joined the others.

"What's that noise," my Pastor asked.

" I don't know. The tire is at eight."

"Pull over now, someone is on the way," he said.

I pulled over into yet another service station. As I am about to close my eyes, out of the corner of my eye I see a tire sign. I was at a full service station that had a tire repair shop. The OPEN light was on. "God you are amazing," I whispered. I opened my door, but before I could get out a man, holding an umbrella, walked over to me. "Wow! What a day for a flat. You look like you headed to church," he said. "We'll have you good to go in a few minutes." Five minutes later, my tire was plugged and I was told to come back after church for repair.

"How much do I owe you?" I asked.

"No charge," the man said. "You are on your way to church."

I went from crying to dancing in the rain, and giving God praise. By the time someone called to ask my location, I joyfully state that the tire had been fixed and that I was on my way. It was a sudden shift, from a trigger that plunged me into grief to a heart filled with gratitude. That day, God assured me that I was never alone, and He will always be with me. Just as I'm not alone, neither are you.

You were not alone yesterday, you are not alone today. And by God's grace, you will not be alone tomorrow, according to Deuteronomy 31:8 (KJV), *"And the Lord, he it is that doth go before thee; he will be with thee, he will not fail thee, neither forsake thee: fear not, neither be dismayed."*

God is with you and when you allow the great God of glory to meet your grief and be present with you in your sorrow, according to 1 Peter 5:7 (KJV), *"Casting all your care upon him; for he careth for you."*

He will reveal that He is mightier than any army of grief, despair, depression, stress, says Psalms 34:17-18 (KJV), *"The righteous cry, and the LORD hearth, and deliverers them out of all their troubles. The LORD is nigh unto them that are of a broken heart; and seventh such as be of a contrite spirit."*

It's time to break your covenant with grief, despair, depression, and stress. Our God is greater and He will give you the strategies to conquer these thieves, allowing you to experience and embrace joy once more. Remember your strategies and use them to be victorious on your daily journey.

> *"For I am persuaded, that neither death, nor life, nor angels, nor principalities, nor powers, nor things present, nor things to come, Nor height, nor depth, nor any other creature, shall be able to separate us from the love of God, which is in Christ Jesus our Lord." Romans 8:38-39 (KJV)*

9 | Glimmering, Glowing and Celebrating

Sometimes we forget that God gave us the capacity to shift our situations and our responses to them. We can be triggered, or we can be glimmering and glowing. Glimmers and glows are new terms used to describe instances that are the opposite of triggers. Glimmers are cues, sensations, happenings to create feelings of joy, calmness and safety while glows are glimmers that last for an extended period of time.

Glimmers and glows bring joy. Joy is the interrupter of grief. Joy turns grief on its head. Joy causes grief to exit. Joy can interrupt grief, anywhere, anytime and anyplace. As we move through the journey, our destination is where there are more days of joy, calm and safety than feelings of grief, pain, and loss. Remembering that God has not given us a spirit of fear, but power, love and a sound mind, as believers we have capacity to move our minds and shift our thoughts.

As previously stated, I am not a clinician, so this is not medical opinion, but based on my personal experiences, as well as observations and conversations with others dealing with grief, I believe that there are some instances and actions that are glimmers for everyone: sunshine, still water, warmth, and smiles.

On my own journey to joy, I discovered and learned my glimmers. I think my glimmers are a reflection of my extroversion and the things that naturally bring me energy and joy. Accordingly, I think that glimmers for introverts can be completely different than glimmers for extroverts. That's why it is important that you find your own glimmers.

But, how do you find or recognize glimmers? Glimmers are your "warm-fuzzy" moments. Moments that elicit spontaneous smiles, moments that bring feelings of calm and joy. You probably already know some of your glimmers, but intentionally tracking these will aid in your journey to joy. Yes, journal these things and then be intentional about practicing them. Once you learn your glimmers, do them. Celebrate your glimmer success and share your joy with others.

My extrovert glimmers and glows include:

People smiling

Calls from my kids

Walks

Journaling

Singing

Shoe shopping

Making a cup of tea with tea leaves (the process is soothing)

Ice cream

A weighted blanket

Hanging with my high school friends

Watching football

Turtles

Some glimmer and glows from my introvert friends include:
Naps
Reading
Puzzles
Drawing
Journaling
Exercising
Learning something new

As you can see there is some overlap between the introverts and extroverts. Once you know your glimmers and glows, be intentional about seeking ways and times to practice and enjoy these moments. Try new things, as you do, you will discover more glimmers. Also, celebrate when a glow blocks a trigger. During the editing phase of this book, I actually experienced this and thought it would be helpful to share.

As I mentioned, my high school friends are "the best." We really love each other. I feel emotionally safe, authentic and loved when I am with them. They are a glow for me. Recently, I attended an alumni event with my classmates, a classmate walked over to where our group was sitting and yelled "Robbie, I heard your husband died. Mine survived." I thought, "What the what! I know she didn't say that." I felt hot, angry, and triggered. However, because I was in a glow, an extended glimmer, I was able to breathe through the moment. I looked at the classmate sitting next to me and said "talk to me about anything now." I could see my classmates were waiting for my reaction. My reaction determined if we were fighting or remaining seated. I chose to keep glowing, and my classmate's hilarious efforts at talking to me worked. In about two-to-three-minutes, I was laughing because he couldn't get it together. Later, another classmate said, she was looking in my eyes and if she thought she saw a hint of a tear, there was going to be "some swinging."

    Later that night I thought, I should have said this or that to her. As I continued to think about the moment, God said, you did what you were suposed to do, enjoy your moment, protect your peace and stay in your journey to joy. Arguing or actually fighting would have been a trigger and a disaster. Maintaining the glow allowed my joy to remain, despite the attempted interruption. To me, that was a win and reason to celebrate. Another win and step forward on my journey to joy.

10 | Are You Ready?

After sharing so much information about my personal journey, I want to share with you a practical roadmap for enjoying life again. This is what has helped me get my mind, my heart, my body, my spirit, and my whole family back on the path of enjoying life. There are many people who know what to do, but will leave it up to you to figure out how. These next three chapters are my "how," and I hope these assist you, bring healing, and reveal to you your very own path to finding joy in life again. So, are you ready?

With the experience of death comes the overwhelming feelings of loss, and loss brings grief. Grief isn't orderly, scheduled, sequential, pretty, neat, predictable, or agreeable. Grief can be ugly, chaotic, unpredictable and overwhelming. I have already told you that grief had to bow to my God, the great Jehovah, the great almighty God, the risen Savior, the king of kings. I defined grief as a painful price of loving. The death of a loved one takes them from your presence. Your grief, your longing, and your desire for them are not optional. Life and death are inevitable parts of the human continuum. Recovery is an option. Either you can remain in a state of grief until you die, physically, emotionally, and spiritually, or you can choose to recover. You can choose to introduce your grief to the great

Jehovah Rapha, the healer. You can choose to live the life God has for you. The choice is yours. Are you ready?

I believe 99% of you reading this book already know that grief can wear you out in every sense — physically, emotionally, spiritually, socially, financially, mentally, and more. In response to the one percent of you who asked, "Really?" the answer is a resounding "Yes!" Rest is vital part of a three-part equation for navigating grief. The three parts are rest, reset and recovery. The remainder of this chapter is dedicated to rest, as it is vital to your journey to joy. The following roadmap can be applied to you and your family members:

Rest Your Heart, Mind, and Body: Allow your heart to find solace in Jesus. Permit Him to heal every hurting part, and don't reclaim that hurt. God is not just a present help. He is present in all aspects — His love, His peace, His comfort, His strength, and His light. All are there to assist and heal us during a season of grief and loss. It's critical to prioritize rest. Yes, actually plan, schedule and commit to rest and self-care in this season. It is critical for your well-being, as our bodies expend a lot of energy during the grieving process.

It's Okay Not to Be Okay for a Season: Understand that it's normal to not be okay for a period, but don't linger in that state. Seek your healing. Know that you are entitled to healing from God, and He desires to heal you. Healing is your birthright as His child.

Continue to Pray: Don't let the enemy or your emotions deceive you into thinking you shouldn't or can't pray. Or worse, that you don't need to. Even when you are angry, stay connected to God through prayer. Pour out your hurt, pain, and grief to Him. Don't retreat from God, run to Him. Tell Him your struggles, remind Him of His promises, and don't hold back. God understands your raw emotions. It's so freeing to tell God what and where it hurts.

I remember laying in my living room floor about two weeks after Verdel died, I was kicking, screaming, beating the floor, hysterical, angry and confused. I did not hold my pain and anger back from God. There have been times I remember getting on my knees to pray and all I could do was cry and groan, no words. But, I know God heard my heart. God has brought us through these seven years and is helping us journey from grief to joy.

Find a Bible App and Soothing Music: Find a Bible app that allows you to listen to God's word when you can't sleep. There are several YouTube channels with soaking worship music which can usher in God's presence while allowing you to rest and sleep. There is nothing like being able to sleep in God's presence when the Word is being read or when worship music is being played. It is a beautiful opportunity to rest in Jesus.

Stay Connected to Your Church: Maintain connections with your Pastors, leaders, small group, or any other support structures your church offers. Let them know how you're doing and when you and your family are struggling. I told my pastor and his wife when I wasn't sleeping, when things were going wrong at work or school, and just how we were doing in general. I did so because I wanted, no I needed them to pray for us.

Children's Grief: It's important to be authentic in your grief, for you and your children. Do not hide your tears and your pain from your children. Normalize the processing of your grief so they will not internalize the processing of their grief. Be honest with them. You can't undo the death, but you can be there for them when they hurt, when they cry, when they struggle, when they open up to talk and when they seek to move forward.

Be open and ready for when they come to you with whatever pain and accompanying emotions (guilt, anger, isolation, depression, or thoughts of suicide) they are having. Do not freak out in that moment (you can do that later). Be stable and solid for them, guide them, hold them, help them or get them help (counseling, medical or other). You can cry later, in those moments, be their strength, comfort and peace. Yes, you can do it! I did it, you can too.

Children and Schools: If your children are affected by the death, please talk to their school principals, counselors and teachers. Let them know what your children are experiencing so that they can be vigilant and on the lookout for any unusual behavior as well as provide additional support. They can be on the lookout for behaviors such as sleeping in class, being withdrawn, outbursts, or not socializing. Alerting school personnel means having an additional set of eyes on your child to ensure they are processing and coping in a healthy way or if more assistance is needed.

Regular Medical Doctor Visits: Ensure you make regular visits to your medical doctor to monitor your nutrition, blood pressure, heart health, weight, exercise routine, sleep patterns, and overall physical well-being. It's essential to maintain a healthy balance.

Grief Counseling: Consider seeing grief counseling for yourself and your family. Professional counselors, including Christian counselors, can provide invaluable support during the emotional healing process. God can work through these professionals to help you on your journey to joy. I went to counseling and my children did also. I believe in God, and had a Christian counselor. God uses people like doctors, lawyers, and counselors to help us toward our goal whether that is physical or emotional need for healing. When there is a spiritual need, God uses a pastor or teacher. God uses people He has called to specific professions.

Take Vitamins: In addition to regular doctor visits, consider taking vitamins to ensure you're getting essential nutrients. Grief can affect your nutrition and overall health. Taking vitamins can help boost your immune system. I found that vitamins B, C and D helped boost my system.

Diet and Nutrition: Journal your meals. Regularly weigh yourself. These habits ensure that you are not under or overeating. Review your eating habits and try to maintain balanced nutrition and hydration. Additionally, there are fresh meal prep and fresh meal delivery services available for reasonable prices, about the same as grocery shopping or eating out. These services can free up time and lessen the feeling of being overwhelmed.

Exercise: Yes, exercise is part of rest. Regular exercise actually assists with clearing the mind of thoughts of grief and pain, replacing with thoughts of calmness and positivity.

Lean On Your Support System: Allow your circle to help you. Put aside pride and let those who care about you assist you in your time of need. Sometimes reaching out for help can be an act of humility. Be open to God to sending blessings and healing your way. I remember a few years after Verdel's passing, I needed some help with some furniture at the house. I wouldn't tell anyone because I didn't want to bother anyone. I just kept trying to figure out how to get it done. One day during this struggle a dear friend called and said "Robbie, the Lord told me to ask, do you need some help moving something? I have my truck and I can help you." I was floored. Stop being someone who doesn't want to reach out because you are being prideful. Strength is asking for help. Wisdom is asking someone who knows and understands. Be strong and wise.

Create a Budget: Establish a budget to manage your finances. Grief can sometimes lead to impulsive spending as a form of therapy, especially for avid shoppers like me. Keeping a budget can help maintain financial stability.

I had packages arriving every day because I was up at night. I shopped everywhere — Amazon, Facebook, Instagram and web sites. The packages would arrive, and I would get the return label and send them back. I would order something and forget I had ordered it. During my grief, I actually purchased the same pair of leopard print heels, twice.

Consult Professionals for Physical Care: If you notice changes in your hair, skin, nails, or scalp due to grief, consult your cosmetologist, hair professional and/or dermatologist. They can provide additional treatments and guidance.

Work and Employment: Inform your workplace leadership about how grief is affecting you, and discuss possible adjustments to your work hours or assignments as needed. Explore options through your employer's Human Resources Department. Some places of employment have sick/vacation banks or vacation donations. Other options may include taking your vacation or sick time, or short-term disability. Even a request under the Americans with Disabilities Act may be appropriate. But, you need to find out what's available to you. Check with your human resources or benefits department about any available employee assistance or benefit programs that may be available to provide free or low cost counseling services.

Allow Yourself to Cry: Cry as often as you feel the need. Crying is a natural, emotional release and you have every right to cry. Holding your emotions in can lead to negative outcomes like health or medical issues, anger outbursts, overeating, withdrawal, or decreased work performance. A few others include elevated blood pressure, anxiety, depression, stress, and delayed healing. None of these are recommended. Tears are part of the process forward.

Address Intimacy Needs: Understand that if your spouse dies there is a strong likelihood that you will miss the physical intimacy you shared. Seek guidance and support to navigate this aspect of grief. Have a plan and boundaries in place to protect your emotional well-being.

This was hard for me (and most people don't talk about it). I not only struggled with insomnia, but longed for the physical touch and presences of my spouse. Being a widow sucked! I had waited for my husband and been faithful. We had an amazing marriage. As a widow, it is imperative I keep myself from situations where things could have easily gone south because I was in a vulnerable place. Once, a friend suggested I go out with this guy. I said nope. My friend declared, "but ya'll would be so cute together." I still said nope. She asked me why. My answer went like this: "He is beyond cute, he's quite sexy and he comes with expectations for more than just dinner activities. I can't do that. I'm in a good space and as my dad would say, 'keep the dragon asleep. If you wake it before it's time, you will have difficulty slaying it'."

Do all you can to keep yourself. Real talk: you may think you know what you can and cannot handle, but remember that you in an unfamiliar and vulnerable position. Think, plan, and be okay saying no. Have options. Have girlfriends or non-romantic guy friends that you can spend time with. Don't trust yourself, trust God.

Intentional Relaxation: Find a relaxation routine that works for you. Schedule and be intentional about engaging in activities like coloring, drawing, journaling, walking, or reading to relax. Don't disconnect from your feelings. Instead, find creative outlets for your emotions.

Remember, healing is a process and you don't have to go through it alone. Reach out for support, lean on your faith, and trust that God is with you every step of the way.

"He maketh me to lie down in green pastures: he leadeth me beside the still waters. He restoreth my soul: he leadeth me in the paths of righteousness for his name's sake. Yea, though I walk through the valley of the shadow of death, I will fear no evil: for thou art with me; thy rod and thy staff they comfort me." Psalm 23:2-4 (KJV)

… STEELE MARTIN

11 | Reset and Recovery

For so many of us the transition or death of a loved one is described as a loss. People say things like, "Sorry for your loss," "in this season of loss," or "as you move through this loss." However, remind yourself that to be absent from the body is to be present from the Lord. For the baptized believers, we have hope that our loved one has simply gone to sleep in Jesus and is resting until the trumpet sounds the rapture.

My father passed about eleven years after my mother. His transition was swift and left me with no time to process what was happening. He had a persistent cough around Resurrection Sunday that wouldn't go away. I remember standing with him at church and he said "Rob I can't shake this cough." I said, "it's probably allergies." He asked me to pray for him. Two weeks later, I was standing beside his hospital bed as he declared, "Either God's going to heal me here or over there, and I'm fine. Either way, I win."

This statement, made by a man who had overcome numerous challenges in life, was a profound expression of faith and trust in God. It showed me that for those who die in Christ, death does not equal loss. It's equal to rounding third base, heading for home plate — a win.

My dad was my hero. He was a strong man. Nothing kept him down. He beat cancer, grief, ADHD and unemployment. He beat having a less than decent education and being a black man in Birmingham, Alabama in the 1960s. He'd beat marijuana.

After my father's transition, my heart was shattered. My mind was devastated. I remember seeking solace from my godmother, crying with rock-sized tears until there was no sound left. My beloved pastor, the late Bishop Heron Johnson, who was in a wheelchair at the time, saw my raw pain, grief, and heartbreak. He prayed with me, wept with me, and reminded me to "hold on to hope." It was during this time that God gave me a comforting fresh in which my father and I walked together. My dad said to me, "Rob, don't worry about the house, the roof leaks." I said, "Yes, sir. He said, "All right. You got this. I'm gonna lay down and I'll meet you over there." I said "Yes, sir." When I looked to my side, he was no longer walking with me, but he was sleeping in the front seat of his light blue and white pickup truck. The inside of the truck was filled with flowers and greenery, it was as if my father had gone to sleep in a beautiful garden. He had peacefully gone to sleep in Jesus. I knew the dream was a sign from God that my daddy had won.

When a loved one dies, the landscape of our life is forever changed. We often say there will always be an empty seat at the table, a hole in our hearts, that our hearts will never heal or we will never love again. The pain is excruciating, especially in the immediate aftermath of their passing.

Fast forward several years. I was in conversation with a grieving parent. They mentioned something that struck a chord in my heart. They talked about how their living child resembled the child they had lost. That simple statement took me back to an experience earlier in the week. A professionally traumatic event occurred at my office. It was an event that left me profoundly hurt and upset. I was deeply affected by it. In that moment of despair, a thought emerged: "I'm going to call my dad and talk to him."

Now, it's essential to understand that I hadn't dialed my dad's number in years. He had passed away years ago, but in real time, I slipped back into that fog where for a fleeting moment, you think you can reach out to your loved one. I couldn't fathom where this sudden thought came from. The truth emerged that I yearned to converse with my dad about this particular event. I desperately needed his insight, advice, and words of wisdom to lean on. As a result, my dad had been on my mind more frequently. I spotted people who looked like him, walked like him, and even spoke like him. I observed strangers doing little quirky things that my Dad did. People I encountered related to or reminded me of my Dad in a myriad of ways.

You see, we tend to focus on what we miss. But in seeing what we miss, we often overlook what is present. What am I getting at? Grief is a relentless thief and robber. It pillages our joy, happiness, hope, stability, and normalcy. But it doesn't stop there. It steals our present. Yes, it steals us away from the ability to be in the present, to savor it, and to exist in it. When we're so preoccupied with the absence of our loved ones, we become blind to the world around us.

So, here's the crux of it. When we're wholly engrossed in missing someone, we inadvertently neglect the wonder still surrounding us. "What is around us?" You may ask. Well, it's God, the good Father, who gently reminds us that reasons for joy still exist. There's hope to be found, moments to smile, and opportunities to laugh. In fact, when you've traversed the jagged terrain of grief and tasted joy and laughter once more, you savor every drop, every second, every iota of happiness, for you never take it for granted. I know I don't. It's not about forgetting the one who died, but honoring their life by resetting yourself and moving forward.

At one point, about a year after my husband's death, three incidents that showed me I had to reset or I was not going to make it:

1. I told my sister that I literally wanted to take my skin off because the pain was unbearable.

2. One day while visiting Verdel's grave, I tried to dig a large hole next to his grave because I intended to stay there.

3. I realized that I was consistently coming home and falling asleep without helping/checking on Jon and Kait.

I was ensnared by the abyss of what I missed, and was missing out on what right in front of me. What quality of life would have existed for me and my children if I lived the rest of my life in that state? I had to willingly reset my mind to my new normal – widowhood.

Resetting didn't mean that I liked it. Resetting meant I refused to be a casualty of grief and lose my remaining life and joy to grief. I challenge you to reset your mind, your thoughts, your words, and your heart. Let me be clear, resetting your mind doesn't mean leaving your loved ones behind or forgetting them. No, your progress, resilience, and forward momentum honors their lives. It's akin to saying, "This person lived, and their impact on my life was so profound that I refuse to let their death overshadow their life."

You can choose to carry on something they loved or excelled at such as volunteering, painting, or gardening. Find something that honors their memory. Scholarships, sponsorships, and donations of any amount are a beautiful opportunity to honor your loved one by aiding someone else.

In resetting, you don't have to relive the day your loved one died over and over again. You've already made it through that day. When resetting, remind yourself of the present date and the fact that you've come this far, you're still alive, and with God's joy as your strength you are going to make it. While tears and pain may come, don't let yourself sink. You have the power to keep moving forward. Reset your mind, your thoughts, your words, and yourself.

Remember:

1. You are alive, and there are so many reasons to find joy. Try joy or gratitude journaling each morning. Write down three things that bring you joy or that you are grateful for. For example, I'm looking at my great nephew's basketball game. It could be as simple as "I didn't cry today."

2. It is okay not to be okay. Your pain, loss and emotions are real and relevant. Do not discount them.

3. It's not okay to stay in that place. Allow yourself to cry, wipe your eyes, and keep moving forward. Baby steps count!

4.Quit quitting. If you quit the journey yesterday, start agin today. You can do this. You can find joy again. We don't quit. We learn, hang on, rest, reset, and move forward.

5. You don't have to be a casualty of grief. Speak life and joy into your future, and don't allow grief to prevail. You deserve healing, and God can provide it.

6. As painful as it is, our loved one's lives ended, but ours has not. I have to keep going, and so do you.

7. Celebrate all wins, big or small. Celebrate victories and enjoy life!

Recovery

Recovery looks different for everyone. I can't describe what your recovery looks like. For me, recovery is about knowing that not every day will be a tear-free day, but most days thoughts of Verdel will come with more smiles than tears. It's about understanding that we can't do this without God's help and trusting Him, even if we don't like His decisions. I still don't like His decision, but I trust Him.

> *"Though he slay me, yet will I trust him: but I will maintain mine own ways before him." Job 13:15* (KJV).

In moments when pain is raw and relentless, remember that God has not abandoned you. He's been there through your pain.

For me, I realize those four eyes looking back at me are full of Verdel (and me) and are reasons for joy. Stretch out on God's promises, hold Him to His word, and you'll find that He is faithful.

As you make progress, let yourself be reminded of how far you've come and use that as fuel to move further. When triggers threaten to set you back, pray for strategies to overcome them. Find new traditions that reflect on memories with smiles rather than tears.

Rather than succumbing to anger, self-pity, or distancing ourselves from the hope and help of God, let's choose to run towards His unfailing hope and assistance. Who better to aid us in our time of need than God himself? It's evident that I can't navigate this journey of grief on my own, or I would have already done so. So, it's a resounding yes to God. Yes, God, I acknowledge that the grief is agonizing. And it's also, yes, God, I surrender the process of healing to you.

Throughout this path of recovery, I've come to realize that I am entitled to my pain, as it is a natural response to Verdel's death. Bluntly, my Dude was freaking awesome and you are darn skippy that there are some days I want to exit the planet because of my intense grief and pain. However, my pain doesn't alter the fact that God maintains His rightful place on the throne. Regardless of when and how our loved ones depart, God's sovereignty endures eternally.

Some days, the recovery journey feels like mountaintop highs of smiles and hopes. Other days, it's valley lows of more tears and pain than the day before. Some days, it's just thanking God for the strength to keep moving forward in the moment.

"He maketh my feet like hinds' feet, And setteth me upon high places." Psalm 18:33 (KJV)

But, if you stay on this journey, somewhere along the way, sooner than later, you will meet joy because you allowed God to meet and defeat your grief. When you meet joy, engage with it, enjoy it fully, and let it fill your life once more.

12 | The Dating Lane

I often refer to dating the "D word." We typically refer to words by the first letter when we don't want to say the word aloud due to their negative or disrespectful connotations. For a widow in a "proper society," dating can indeed feel like the "D word" because it introduces numerous variables that can easily disrupt the delicate balance of an already unsteady life.

It may sound absurd, but the first time I realized I was single and eligible to date, I was overwhelmed with emotion. I vividly remember the moment as I drove home on Highway 150 after completing paperwork for an outpatient procedure.

The paperwork asked for marital status and presented only two options: married or single. Widow was not an option. I stared at the paperwork, grappling with my identity. I knew I wasn't married, but I hadn't truly contemplated what it meant to be single. The word single with all its implications of solitude, had not crossed my mind until that moment. I hadn't mentally arrived at that point yet.

As I drove, tears welled up in my eyes, blurring my vision. Those tears soon turned into uncontrollable sobs, forcing me to pull over because I could no longer see through my veil of emotions. I was in no condition to continue driving. Why was I sobbing so hard? It hit me like a tidal wave that single people actually did this thing called dating.

It's one thing to date your spouse, keep the spark of romance, excitement, and love alive in your marriage. But it's an entirely different experience to be a single person navigating the world of dating. I hadn't been on a date with anyone other than my beloved in over twenty years. I never envisioned myself with anyone else, but Verdel. So, I wondered in disbelief, "Lord, why am I here? Why did this happen? I don't like this. I don't know what to do. You love me, God, so why am I facing this?"

With the notion of the "D word" came another significant word: timing. I grappled with the concept of when to start dating. Verdel had been an honorable man, and it was crucial for me to honor his memory in my heart, mind, and daily life.

Looking back seven years later, I wonder if my commitment to honor was indeed honoring or a way of avoiding the inevitable. What did that honor look like, and how did my decision to honor Verdel affect me as a young and very much alive widow? Was it genuine honor, or was I simply evading moving forward?

Amidst all the conversations I had about dating, one of the most impactful ones was with my daughter. We were in the bathroom, causally chatting while I brushed her hair. Kait, was an eleventh-grader at the time, and I had been a widow for four years. We were laughing and discussing her hair when she looked in the mirror and said, "Mom, you taking too long. What are you doing?"

Confused, I asked her to explain. Kait said, "You're not doing anything You're wasting time. Jon is already gone to college, and I'm leaving, too. You'll be by yourself."

Her words hit me like a ton of bricks, and she continued, "Don't ask Jon to come back home because he lives in Tuscaloosa. Mom, I want you to have a life. I don't want you to be lonely. You need to try. Dad would want you to be happy."

I leaned against the door, tears streaming down my face. I managed to say, "Okay, little girl. I understand what you're saying. I'll try. But whether I do or not, don't worry about me. This is your time to go and be amazing. Either way, I'll be okay."

I was incredibly grateful for her wisdom and straightforwardness, which reminded me that I was more than just their mother. I was Robbie, and I was alive. Until God called me home, I had every right to enjoy life and dating could be a part of it. It was a powerful awakening, and I was thankful for the pep talk that only Kait could deliver.

I talked to Jon a few days later, and casually mentioned my conversation with his sister to gauge his thoughts. "'Bout time you think about it and don't find no lame. Dad was an OG and you deserve that," Jon said. "Yeah me and Kait been talking about." Wide-eyed that my kids are getting me together, my response was, " Well, okay, I'll keep that in mind." And I have. No lames for me.

However, not all conversations about dating were as positive. About three years into widowhood, I found myself in a situation where someone needed a reminder about boundaries.

We were at a large dinner gathering, enjoying each other's company and sharing laughter. I casually mentioned that a gentleman had approached me politely, asking if I was married and requesting my phone number. A married friend at the table, who was close to all of us and knew Verdel, overheard and immediately chimed in. "Oh no, you can't do that." I looked at him, taken aback, and asked whom he was talking to. I continued, "Do you even understand what it's like to consider dating someone after losing your spouse?"

He responded, and I retorted, "No, you don't." I went on to explain that the mere act of contemplating whether I should give someone my number triggered a flood of thoughts and fears. At over forty with two kids, the dating pool seemed limited. I was battling thoughts of loss, imagining scenarios where a new partner might die before me. I was caught between fear and possibilities. So, if I chose to share my number, it was an act of courage. I told him to either applaud that decision or simply remain quiet. "Now, please pass the bread," I said realizing that I needed something in my mouth before I continued. Sometimes people need reality check, especially when they lack insight into another person's experience.

These experiences made me realize the importance of setting boundaries and asserting my own agency in my journey as a widow. Dating was my choice, my prerogative, and my responsibility. In the end, it isn't about other people's opinions. It is about what felt right for me, and I was determined to navigate this new chapter in my life on my terms.

So, you may be wondering, have I ventured into the dating lane?

I believe the answer is yes. I'm open to being approached, going out, and embracing my singleness. Somewhere along this healing journey, I've moved from widowhood to single hood. It's akin to the relationship between Naomi and Ruth. Both were widows, but Ruth navigated life with openness to God's plan for her.

During the first several years, whenever a male approached me or made a respectful and courteous attempt to start a conversation, my immediate response was always, "I'm a widow." It was like a reflex, a defense mechanism signaling that I wasn't ready for anything else. Looking back, I realize they might have found my response abrupt or bewildering. There's one memorable incident when a guy tried to strike up a conversation with me at the library. My reflex kicked in and I responded with my usual, I'm a widow, and promptly exited the scene. Later, he told one of my longtime male friends, "Robbie is attractive, but I think she's a bit eccentric." No, I am not eccentric. I was simply trying to navigate the uncertain waters of my next chapter.

Later, there was this gentleman who approached me with impeccable politeness, and when he started the conversation, I cut him off quickly with my I'm a widow defense. He said, "Okay, that means you're single. What would you like me to do with this information?" I hadn't prepared for such a response, and it caught me off guard. In my haste, I replied, "I'm just making sure you are aware." He countered with, "Alright, I'm just making sure you are aware that I'd like to get your number." Surprisingly he was two steps ahead, and I was stuck in a conversation. I found myself curious about where this might lead.

God has mended my heart in a beautiful way throughout this recovery journey, surpassing my wildest expectations. I've placed my trust in Him, and He has remained unwaveringly faithful. God performed what only He could do. Simultaneously, I did my part by allowing my grief to intersect with my greater faith in God. I prayed earnestly, sought therapy, confided in my loved ones, consulted with my pastor, and held countless conversations with God. I beseeched Him to perform the miracle of healing my broken heart, the heart that I'd been constantly rubbing due to its pain. I asked for strength to embrace life fully, to venture out alone or with friends, regardless of gender, and to relish in the experience. God granted me renewed strength to find joy once more, to engage in life's pleasures, whether that meant sharing moments with colleagues, my children, my friends, or making new friends.

I prayed to God, saying, "I'm still alive and I want to live. I want to experience joy and happiness in my now and my next."

My current dates don't necessarily equal marriage. For me, they signify a willingness to get to know someone and grant them a space, perhaps a place in my life. On my journey to joy, I am in a place where dates equal companionship, not necessarily relationship. My discussions about marriage are ongoing with God. I genuinely don't know if I desire to marry again. God, in His infinite kindness and patience, listens to my heartfelt reflections. I've not actively prayed for a husband at this stage, but maybe I will in the future.

Presently, I'm content with dating. Not everyone may resonate with my stance, and that's perfectly fine. What works for me may not work for others. Each person's journey is unique, and it's important to engage in a conversation with God to discern the path that aligns with your heart and desires. I am on a journey of recovery and joy, and with every step, I grow stronger. The road ahead may hold surprises, and perhaps God's plan for me involves another "I do." That's for the days ahead. Today, I'm proud of myself for taking significant steps, for giving my number to a man, for agreeing to a date, for dressing up, for having a great time, and for returning home safely by eleven o'clock in the evening and getting the "Hope you are home safely" or "Had a great time and hope you say yes to another date" text.

That is progress, effort, intentional behavior, and a conscious choice to engage in joy and excitement. It also is choosing to live and to break free from all anyone's thoughts and doing what works for me. That is trusting God for my now and my next!

Before I conclude this chapter, I'd like to share my roadmap for "merging into the dating lane." If, at some point, you decide you're ready to venture into the dating world, consider these insights:

1. Remember, you're starting from a standstill. Once you found and dated your spouse, you probably never expected to return to the dating scene. Like a vehicle that's been in a wreck

and repaired, you've changed, and you've aged a bit. Approach and merge into the dating lane with caution.

2. Recognize your immense value. You are fearfully and wonderfully made. You possess beauty, kindness, and thoughtfulness. You deserve to embrace joy and happiness.

3. Pray for your potential spouse. Observe them closely. Understand that people in this phase of life are who they are, and it can be challenging to change them. Trust your instincts and don't ignore red flags.

4. If you desire marriage, pray for your potential partner. Be honest with yourself and God about your desires.

5. Enjoy your current season while keeping an open heart and mind. Try not to be anxious. Don't rush things. Trust that God will honor your prayers and either bless you according to your desires or reveal His better plan for you.

6. Be prepared for rejection. Understand that you won't be everyone's cup of tea, and that's perfectly fine. Your life experiences have likely shifted your perspective, and that's okay, too.

7. Be approachable. It's okay to engage in polite conversation. A simple hello doesn't commit you to a Saturday night date. It's merely a friendly gesture.

8. Most importantly, savor the present moment. Relish the joy of your life. Live every day to the fullest.

Psalm 118:24 (KJV) — *"This is the day which the Lord hath made; we will rejoice and be glad in it."* — has gained profound meaning for me, as I've learned to live each day with joy and gratitude. I've found reasons to be joyful, and I've witnessed God's grace in my life. If He did it for me, I have no doubt He will do it for you, too. Stay on your recovery journey, and you'll discover joy again.

LEARNING TO LIVE AGAIN

Bonus | Thriving During Holidays and Special Occasions

We can be our own source of frustration, particularly during the holidays or special occasions. We set our expectations and make to do lists. So many times it is our heart's desire to make the holidays and celebrations exactly like they were before our loved one passed away. We know our loved ones are not physically present, but the least we can do is "make Christmas like it was when mama was alive," "have it set out just like granny did every Resurrection Easter Sunday," or "make sure the ribs are fall off the bone tender like daddy did."

Below are some holiday strategy suggestions to aid in your journey to joy. Choose the method that best suits you or your current situation.

Accepting the Changes Between Then and Now

We can easily traverse from enjoying the holidays memories and special occasions with our loved ones to creating frantic panic, frustration, anxiety, or anger and run the risk of ruining the day. I was constantly beating myself up because I couldn't get Christmas right. To me, getting Christmas right meant my "now" had to be my "was" — my present had to be my past. Even though both my parents were deceased, I was trying with all my might to make Christmas look, feel, smell, and taste just as it did when they were alive. I spent so many Christmases frustrating myself and probably those around me. My tree, dinner, nor my shopping weren't right.

Suddenly my tree wasn't right because it wasn't decorated the way my dad decorated our childhood tree. I later realized the tree was an issue after my dad's death because of my strong Christmas memories. At the time, I'd been married for more than ten years and had multiple Christmas trees. I'd never given them much thought until after my father passed. The tree became a trigger for me because I had to get it just right.

As I looked back over this, I realized I was looking for the tree from my childhood. As I traversed from joyful childhood memories towards frustration and anxiety, I wished I could turn my present into my past when my father was alive. Trying and failing every year must have frustrated those around me.

And then there was the fact that my dinner "wasn't right," particularly the dressing. My dad made the best dressings, oyster and Hawaiian bread dressing. Every year I would try to get the taste right. In my mind right was not defined as good or acceptable, right was defined as "just like Dad's." I remember sitting at the dinner table. Everyone was enjoying my dressing.

"Oh, Robbie, this dressing is good," my grandma said. My sourpuss response was, "It's not right. It's not like dad's."

My Dude, as only he could do, said, "It's not your dad's, it's yours, and it tastes great! I'll take seconds." In that moment, Verdel's response freed me from my own bondage that had arrested me year after year. The dressing didn't have to be just like my Dad's. It was mine and it was good. It was really good!

Later that night, I began to let Verdel's words sink into my brain and my heart, the dressing was mine, and it was good. The dressing didn't have to be like dad's to be right. The remainder of Christmas break, I examined my over-the-top, extra effort to make the dressing like my dad and realized I was making myself and everyone around me miserable when it came to even discussing the dinner menu. I decided I had enough of "getting it right." The following year, I suggested we have something completely different for Christmas dinner. One year we had fish, french fries, coleslaw, baked beans, cakes, pies, and ice cream. No dressing! Everybody enjoyed it. We made another wonderful new memory and started a new tradition for Christmas dinner. We were enjoying life and engaging in joy.

You don't have to do things "just like" they were done in the past. It's okay to create new memories and new traditions. Your most important assignment, task and number one on your to do list is to take care of yourself and be a blessing to those that are present. Do what brings you joy in the season. So what if you don't get the sweet potato pie like Big Mama or Granny. It's okay. I promise you don't even have to have pie, as long as you do what makes you happy.

Consider your now and your was. What's the one thing you need to allow God to transition from you? Allow God to meet your grief and be reminded that God is greater than your grief. Allow Him to free you of this bondage of trying to fit your past into your now. What are some new traditions you can engage in or embrace during this Christmas or other holiday season? What are some new things that you can experience that will bring you joy and make new memories?

Scheduling Joy

Make it a point to allocate time for joy in your life. This could involve writing it on your paper calendar, adding it to your Outlook calendar, pinning it to your wall calendar, placing a reminder on the fridge, or setting an alarm on your phone. Choose the method that suits you best. Actually schedule dedicated time for activities that truly uplift your spirits. Whether it's taking a leisurely walk, indulging in your all-time favorite movie, tackling an engaging puzzle, or connecting with your Bestie over a FaceTime call. Give joy official recognition by scheduling it. Scheduling joy serves not only as a source of anticipation, especially during challenging moments, but also a reminder that self-care should be your foremost priority.

Drawing from my own experiences, my calendar remains brimming with events year-round. From Valentine's Day in February to Mother's Day in May, our wedding anniversary in June, and even October, the month Verdel passed. It encompasses luncheons, massages, painting classes, store grand openings, market visits, restaurant launches, plays, shopping, and sporting events. Essentially, a wide array of delightful activities populate my calendar and nurture positive expectations as I navigate the complex world of widowhood. As I compose this book, I look forward to my great-nephew's basketball games, numerous Christmas and holiday gatherings, vacation time with my college-bound children, days designated for serene walks, moments reserved for writing, and two precious days set aside for indulging in my all-time favorite treat, ice cream. The knowledge that enjoyable moments are on the horizon helps me combat loneliness and sadness, especially during various holidays and occasions. Trust me, it may require some practice, but rest assured, you CAN achieve it!

Distinguishing Solitude from Loneliness

It's essential to grasp the fundamental difference between being alone and feeling lonely. Picture this scenario: You find yourself meandering through an open market, entirely on your own. While there are vendors to engage in conversation with and perhaps other shoppers to interact with, what genuinely captivates you is the mesmerizing spectacle of the market itself. Your mind teems with observations and thoughts, and every moment becomes enchanting. Loneliness? That's nowhere in sight. It's an experience that's intriguing, thought-provoking, and time-consuming in the best possible way. It brings you unadulterated joy.

Now, let's address loneliness. Loneliness isn't just about physical solitude. It encompasses an emotional void, a yearning for connection and companionship. It's the pang in your heart when you miss your loved ones. However, being alone doesn't automatically translate to loneliness. You can revel in your own company and still feel content, engaged, and joyful.

Embracing the Present Moment

Brace yourself because what I'm about to say is both challenging and essential. Your loved one is gone. No matter how hard we try to recreate the past, they can't return. Your life will never be the same as it once was. Nevertheless, this doesn't mean it can't be filled with peace, hope, love, laughter, and joy. We honor our past by cherishing those beautiful memories forever etched in our hearts. However, what truly matters is the present.

Ask yourself, "What does my present look like" Is it a peaceful place where cherished memories coexist harmoniously with new ones? Or is it reminiscent of your past, where you constantly berated yourself for not getting everything just right? You don't need to replicate your "now" to match your "then." You can create new memories and traditions while cherishing the old ones. Your primary focus should be on taking care of yourself and being a source of joy for those present with you.

As the holiday season approaches, contemplate your "now" and your "then." Is there something from your past that you need to let go of? Allow God to assist you in transitioning from the past into the present. Embrace new traditions, experience joy, and prioritize being kind to yourself and your loved ones. Remember, it's perfectly acceptable if your sweet potato pie doesn't quite measure up to Big Mama's. Your happiness is what truly matters. P.S. After all Jesus is the reason for the season!

Take a moment to reflect on the things that have brought you joy in your life. Perhaps you were a puzzle enthusiast as a child but haven't had the opportunity to revisit that passion. Well, puzzles should certainly top your list. Once you've compiled your joy list, remember the internet can be a great ally. Discover those joyful activities in your area and dive right in. Many of these events are free, and just like my experience at a vegan tasting, you might find yourself alone but far from lonely. Identify what brings you joy, schedule it, engage in it, and immerse yourself in the pure, unadulterated joy of living. You CAN do it. I'm cheering for you.

ADDENDUM

As I finalized this book, I went to visit Rock Star for her university's Family Weekend. At one point, she and I separated. I was charged with going to the bookstore to checkout the new hoodies while she went back to her dorm room. In the bookstore, I shopped, oohing and ahhing at all the merchandise. Then, I ran across the "Mom" items — the mom T-shirt, sweatshirt, hoodie, mugs and key chains. Grabbing several items, I circled back to see what other items I could find.

I walked into the "Dad" section. My heart jumped into my chest. I knew Verdel would be so proud and excited for our daughter's college selection, success and enjoyment. I held onto the "Dad" sweatshirt as the tears welled in my eyes. I felt triggered. I reminded myself to breathe through it and remember the present. I thought "Verdel would be proud and enjoy this time." I will enjoy this, too. I knew Verdel would purchase and proudly wear his Dad items. So me, my tears, my smile and my mom items made our way to the counter, I purchased my Mom items and we enjoyed Family Weekend!

We are living again. We are winning the battle against grief. We have joy. We are doing it, on this journey, one day at a time. So can you!

STEELE MARTIN

ABOUT THE AUTHOR

Robbie, is the daughter of the late Robert and Gwen Steele and wife of the late Verdel Martin. She decided to partner with life and joy.

She is the loving and probably over-protective Momma Bear of two college students know as Rocket and Rock Star. Robbie is an active member of Bethesda Apostolic Church and believes in leaving the world a better place one step or shoe at a time.

Robbie is a baptized believer with a heart for those dealing with grief. Her own journey of widowhood led her to write this book. Initially, she thought she was on a never-ending journey of grief, but realized not only did she want to enjoy her life again and have joy, but both were still accessible. Now she wants everyone wrestling to grief to know that joy can be theirs again. They do not have to be causalities of grief. Joy and hope are available.

The Birmingham, Alabama native is a dynamic speaker, mentor, and thought-partner.

STEELE MARTIN

Made in the USA
Columbia, SC
25 November 2023